Made to Lead

Finding a Virtuous Wife in Sodom

By

Robert Cossins

About the Author

Rob Cossins is first and foremost a Christian, a follower of Jesus. Though his is an imperfect walk, his faith informs every important decision he makes. Over the past twenty years, Robert has had the opportunity to counsel numerous men regarding life, faith, career and marriage. He believes God calls men to be as intentional regarding their marriage as they are regarding other important areas in life, and encourages men to pursue *intentional* living. He believes the marital decision one of the most crucial decisions a man will ever make. Made well, it enables a man to fulfill his life's mission; made poorly, it's debilitating and immensely destructive to family, church, children, and even society. Though marriage is a lifetime commitment before God, it's not an eternal one, ending at the death of either spouse; however, though the marital vows cease at death, it's a vow before God that *clearly changes eternity*. He encourages men to marry well, proceeding carefully, and always seeking God's discernment. Rob is a man with many scars, who's willing to openly share what he's learned, just as he's learned from others.

Over his years of working with men, it became apparent that, much to their detriment, most men receive very little instruction or advice regarding selecting a good wife so, in 2012, he established the Made to Lead Institute specifically designed to provide men *straight talk* about how to fulfill their life's mission, how to marry well, and how to improve their marriage. He delivers these materials via seminar and has completed the first in a planned series of books entitled, *Made to Lead: Finding a Virtuous Wife in Sodom.*

Robert previously served as CEO of a privately-held technology firm he founded nearly twenty years ago, a firm which delivered over a million hours of software consulting and engineering services during his ownership tenure. He still consults with start-up to mid-sized businesses on strategic issues.

Cossins is the named inventor on several patents related to geographical information systems and has had his admittedly abstruse research on computer modeling of complex systems published. Over time, people have become more important to him, and technology less. To that end, he served one of his alma maters for over a decade as a founding member of a committee seeking to better prepare computer science graduates for the real world. He has spoken in inner-city high schools to encourage disadvantaged students to prepare for their future and to break the cycle of dysfunction in their families. He currently serves as the director of his church's board and in various ministry-related roles.

Cossins enjoys water sports, hiking, hunting, long-distance target shooting, making things with his hands, and off-road motorcycling. He loved football until it became a penalty to make a good play. He is fascinated by history and is a devotee of Austrian economics.

Rob may be contacted at cossins@made-to-lead.com. To receive more information on his organization, please visit www.made-to-lead.com.

Disclaimer

The information contained in this book is intended for educational purposes only. It is sold and provided with the understanding that neither the author nor publisher is engaged in rendering legal advice, counseling, or any other professional advice. The information herein is not a substitute for professional care or counsel. The author is not a licensed counselor.

No representations, either expressed or implied, are made or given regarding the use of the information provided. The author is in no way liable for any use or misuse of the material.

This book deals with marriage and sexuality in direct terms. It is intended for mature readers.

MADE TO LEAD: FINDING A VIRTUOUS WIFE IN SODOM
Copyright © 2013 by Robert Cossins
First Edition: March, 2013
First Printing: December, 2013

All rights reserved. No part of this manuscript may be reproduced or transmitted in any form or by any means, electronic or mechanical, including photocopying, recording, or by any informational storage or retrieval system, except by a reviewer who may quote brief passages in a review to be printed or published electronically, without permission in writing from the author. Although the author and publisher have researched all sources to ensure the accuracy and completeness of the information contained herein, we assume no responsibility for errors, inaccuracies, omissions or any inconsistency of the materials. Any slights of people or organizations are completely unintentional.

Cover design by JartStar. Adapted from the painting entitled *Saint George and the Dragon* by Pieter Pauwel Rubens, 1620.

Original *Leader* pencil sketch by Dino Wise.

Published by the Made to Lead Institute

ISBN 978-0615939483

Unless otherwise noted, Scripture quotations are from the Holy Bible, New International Version, copyright © 1973, 1978, 1984 by the International Bible Society.

Created in the United States of America.

ACKNOWLEDGMENTS

I thank the many men over the past two decades who've invited me into their lives and let me walk with them through difficult times. You are my friends and have taught me much.

I further acknowledge those performing honest research in fields that help us better understand men, women, and how they relate to one another. Their insights and findings have greatly refined my thinking, particularly the thoughts and ruminations of Vox Day, truly an original thinker. If he wasn't so busy writing epic fantasy, he might well have tackled a similar project, with great aplomb I'm quite sure. Additionally, the blogger Dalrock is an accomplished miner of historical statistics and always provides valuable and illuminating commentary.

I wish to thank those who read and commented on early versions of this manuscript: my long-time pastor, Joel Atwell; my friend for over forty years, Terry Campbell; and my own lovely bride. Though their views don't necessarily fully reflect my own, I greatly valued their input. I also thank those who've attended the Made to Lead class and provided their valuable feedback.

I also wish to thank my oldest daughter, Jacy, first for being such a wonderful daughter and, second, for giving me permission to share some of our personal correspondence in the "Raising Your Daughters" chapter.

I dedicate this book to my Lord and Savior, Jesus Christ of Nazareth – the Word, the Creator, the Judge, the Perfect Leader. He would not release me until I wrote these words; if it's in His will, may He use them powerfully and widely as I pray:

Heavenly Father, may the following words fully reflect Your Truth. Please open men's hearts to receive them in the manner in which they were intended. May you especially give the suffering man all discernment in their use, guiding him to apply his newfound knowledge to the betterment of himself, his family, and Your Kingdom. Redeem his mistakes and draw him and his family to you. Give him the grace and power to break any cycles of dysfunction, leaving an inheritance of wisdom for his children and his children's children. Always restrain the evil one from sowing confusion. Give us courage to change, to improve, to seek truth. Remove the scales from our eyes, giving us eyes to see, to honestly observe, and provide our minds with clear understanding of what we see. Provide us sufficient courage to forge ahead alone if necessary, but we seek the blessing of your strong right hand, that you might bring brothers beside us, walking shoulder-to-shoulder in Your good will, that we might finish Your race well and together. Draw us to Your will. Form us with Your Potter's hand. Enable us to fight the good fight and enter Your pleasure. In Jesus' powerful name, I lift these requests through the power of His shed blood. May we walk authentically in His perfect footsteps. Amen and amen.

Table of Contents

Acknowledgments vi
Preface 1
Preparation 14
Marry Well 22
Biblical Marriage 30
Avoiding the Scourge of Divorce 42
Sexual Market Value 53
Hypergamy 62
Partner Count Matters 69
Career and Credentials 79
She Really Does Think Differently Than You Do 87
Attracting Quality Women 92
Her Actions Speak Louder Than Her Words 100
Raising Your Daughters 109
Triage 133
Conclusion 143

PREFACE

As iron sharpens iron, so one man sharpens another.[1]
— *King Solomon*

It is a reality of life that men are competitive and the most competitive games draw the most competitive men. That's why they are there - to compete. The objective is to win fairly, squarely, by the rules - but to win. And in truth, I've never known a man worth his salt who in the long run, deep down in his heart, didn't appreciate the grind, the discipline. There is something in good men that really yearns for discipline and the harsh reality of head-to-head combat.[2]
— *Coach Vince Lombardi*

This is a book for men, Christian men.

---

[1] Proverb 22:17
[2] Vince Lombardi and Vince Lombardi, Jr., *What it Takes to Be Number One* (Nashville: Thomas Nelson, Inc., 2012), page 17.

Preface

Among the most debilitating decisions a man can make is to marry poorly. Conversely, one of the most enabling decisions a man can make is to marry well or not at all. If you marry, marry well. This book is designed first and foremost to help you do precisely that, and it will also help those already married, whether they married well or less than well.

It's foundational to understand that God made men to lead, but, for men to lead well, they must be leading toward defined goals, to be on a mission, to be operating with a purpose, a plan. The effectiveness of a man on a mission compared to the wandering, hapless man can be illustrated by comparing a modern fighter jet and a toy balsa wood glider: One will fulfill its purpose, imposing the will of its pilot on the atmosphere to achieve its goals, the other but a cheap toy for childhood amusement, its actions controlled by its environment, by the very wind that will eventually destroy it. As with the fighter jet, the man on a mission exerts his good will against the world in pursuit of his goals and will lead effectively. Those in his sphere – family, church, business, society – will benefit greatly, as will the man himself.

The purpose of the *Made to Lead* series of books is straightforward: To encourage men to seek their mission, to understand and execute their God-ordained responsibilities to the best of their abilities, and to help prepare them to do so. Men that do this (and do it well) live exciting, effective, fulfilled lives worthy of emulation. Today's generation cries out for your considered leadership; from before the womb, tomorrow's generations cry out, *cry out*, for a generation of godly leaders, clearing and marking the Good Path in preparation for their time. Let us not disappoint either the present or the future.

Though these books are written in submission to God, they are nothing if not rebellious books. They rebel against a culture spawned and spread by our mortal Enemy. Though he's operating with an expiration date, he and his minions are running to and fro, working to destroy all that is good, seeking to substitute his lies and half-truths for God's Truth. Herein we shall seek out and expose his lies about marriage with prejudice. Tragically, throughout church history, some of the most dangerous and destructive lies have come packaged with the compromised churches' seal of approval. Church endorsed lies will be attacked with a particular vengeance, for little is more destructive to a Christian than confusion sown by the church. But before we get started in earnest, we must pour a foundation, and then we shall get very, very practical, for this is a boots on the ground book.

> *Little is more destructive to a Christian than confusion sown by the church.*

Just as the Apostle Peter warned the nascent church, "Save yourselves from this corrupt generation,"[3] each generation in turn must turn away from sin and toward God's truth, then reflect His Good News back into the broader culture. Oftentimes the opposite is the case, both historically and today, with many churchgoers merely marking time rather than following the Lord. The Apostle Paul described those holding to a false or hollow faith thusly: "To the pure, all things are pure, but to those who are corrupted and do not believe, nothing is pure. In fact, both their minds and consciences are corrupted. They claim to know God, but by their actions they deny him. They are detestable, disobedient and unfit for doing anything good."[4] His words are particularly applicable in

---

[3] Acts 2:40
[4] Titus 1:15

our time to those steeped in modern, feminist-derived "churchianity," the pretense of Christianity but without the true Christ or His plain-spoken word. Just as the Lord made the scales fall from Paul's eyes,[5] we must invite Him to remove the scales from ours so that we might see with honest eyes.

If you are a churchian, or even a genuine Christian trying to reconcile the Bible with the modern "isms" in which you have been indoctrinated, these books may well drive your mind into cognitive dissonance, a confused state brought on by holding two incongruous beliefs simultaneously. When genuinely confused, most men's minds demand a resolution and, in this particular case, there are two obvious paths: The first and best path is through unrelenting investigation until the truth is ultimately understood, but the easier and more commonly utilized alternative is simply to allow your mind to hold two mutually exclusive opinions, taking some care to never draw upon them simultaneously.

Do you recall when you were first told that Santa Claus was not real? In that moment you almost assuredly experienced cognitive dissonance. I certainly did. My only slightly older aunt, lacking any good motivation whatsoever, informed me of the dark truth, during our Christmas celebration no less. I'll never forget arguing with her, then going to my parents for their backing. Not wanting to let loose of the innocent lie, they assured me that Santa did exist. In complete and utter confusion, back and forth I went between my parents and my aunt, two trusted parties with diametrically opposed positions, only one of which could be true. Either Santa existed or he did not. Of course, my aunt was proven correct in the end but, though I'm probably in the minority, when I finally understood that Santa did not exist, a small seed of distrust was planted in my mind. If Santa was a lie, what other lies had my parents told me? Though my

---

[5] Acts 9:18

parents were proven trustworthy countless times through the years, as for me, I resolved to never play the Santa game with my kids, innocent though it might be; I wanted them to trust me implicitly in everything. (By the way, thanks for that bike back in '66 Santa; it was awesome! The first time I rode it was on an ice-covered grocery store parking lot on Christmas Day, never donning a helmet or knee pads or elbow pads, yet I miraculously survived to tell the tale.)

Another straightforward example of cognitive dissonance is from the movie *The Matrix*. Neo's character was presented a choice by Morpheus, to take the Red Pill and seek the Truth or the Blue Pill to continue living the Lie, a comfortable Lie. "For wide is the gate and broad is the road that leads to destruction, and many enter through it,"[6] is how Jesus described the way of the Lie, always the seemingly easy choice, but Neo chose the Red Pill, and the adventure began. Choosing the Red Pill was the seemingly risky choice, one that he certainly regretted at times. Still, choosing to seek the Truth - to walk through the "narrow gate"[7] - is always the right choice from an eternal perspective.

The single biggest Red Pill moment in any Christian man's life must be his decision to follow Jesus, the decision that changes literally everything. Many Jewish leaders believed in Jesus but "would not confess their faith for fear they would be put out of the synagogue."[8] Unfortunately, many Christians follow in the Jewish leaders' footsteps, those who "loved praise from men more than praise from God."[9] Choosing the Red Pill must include the decision to follow God with one's whole heart, to seek the Truth no matter where it leads, no matter how uncomfortable, no matter how against

---

[6] Matthew 7:13
[7] Ibid.
[8] John 12:42
[9] John 12:43

the grain, no matter the cost. May the followers of Jesus always choose the Red Pill and seek the Truth, letting God remove the blinding scales from their eyes.[10] But to separate Truth from Lies one must seek to understand things as they really exist. Sadly, most in today's society take Morpheus' Blue Pill metaphorically, and many take all manner of actual pills of various colors, numbing themselves from the realities of life, reducing their ability to distinguish fantasy from reality.

When it comes to the relationships between men and women, the equalitarians bark that they should be treated as equal in every respect. Feminists often deny even the existence of gender differences; however, unchained from the zeitgeist, even the most simpleminded can readily observe this is merely feminist fantasy. Men and women are unequal in just about every respect: height, weight, strength, speed, endurance, expected lifespan, aptitude, interests, hobbies, accomplishments, sex drive, ability to nurture, the manner in which they think and solve problems, and so forth and so on, ad infinitum. Indeed, there are no two people ever created who are equal in every respect. Equality is truly a fantasy and, as the West shall learn, treating unequal things as equal is irrational and counterproductive in the extreme. Western man is conditioned in feminism and equalitarianism from an early age, so steeped in its tenants that most have become emasculated, a conditioning with results perhaps best described by C. S. Lewis:[11]

And all the time—such is the tragi-comedy of our situation—we continue to clamour for those very qualities we are rendering impossible. You can hardly open a periodical without coming across the statement that what our civilization needs is more 'drive', or dynamism, or self-sacrifice, or 'creativity'. In a sort of ghastly simplicity we remove the organ and demand the function. We make

---

[10] Acts 9:18
[11] C.S. Lewis, *The Abolition of Man* (C. S. Lewis Pte, Ltd., 1944), page 26.

men without chests and expect of them virtue and enterprise. We laugh at honour and are shocked to find traitors in our midst. We castrate and bid the geldings be fruitful.

Emasculated men can't lead even themselves, let alone a family and beyond, so, no matter our present conditioning, Christian men must find their courage, their "chests," and seek to live authentic Christian lives, for healthy families and effective churches must be led by men. The Apostle Paul couldn't have been clearer: "I do not permit a woman to teach or have authority over a man."[12] He does not qualify his statement, nor does he make it conditional in any way (though many seek to apply conditions or narrow his proscription.)[13] Even if you wholly disagree with my "narrow" reading of this verse, you would do well to at least consider the ubiquitous, easily observable evidence emanating from today's culture. Is America's a healthy culture? If not, why not? Has it ever been healthy? If so, what has changed?

> *Christian leaders compromise on this biblical principal at their peril because all organizations require good leadership and, hear me well, strong men simply do not follow women.*

The church is not immune from the culture of its members and, indeed, feminism has taken root not just in the world but in most all churches and families, leaving them mere ineffective shells of what God intended. Christian leaders compromise on this biblical

---

[12] 1 Timothy 2:12a

[13] See Gilbert Bilezikian, *Beyond Sex Roles: What the Bible Says about a Woman's Place in Church and Family* (Grand Rapids, MI: Baker Academic, 2006) for a thorough, if flawed, treatment of the positive case.

principal at their peril because all organizations require good leadership and, hear me well, *strong men simply do not follow women.* One need only observe adolescent males being raised by single mothers to understand that even most *boys* refuse to follow female leadership when it is unchained from adult male enforcement, even leadership from their own mothers. A matriarchal culture is a culture of disorder and dysfunction, America's inner cities providing sufficient evidence to draw proper conclusions, with black out-of-wedlock birth rates exceeding four out of five in some entire states, and with other races following in their footsteps.[14] It was not always so. To put this massive shift into proper perspective, in 1960, in a day before the birth control pill, the Plan B pill, or legal abortion, in the U.S. only one out of twenty children were born to unmarried mothers. Today that number is approaching eight out of twenty births, almost forty percent, an 800% increase over that period of time.[15] How high would this number be without abortion, whether chemical or surgical? The fruits of feminism are bitter; they reek of death.

In many churches feminism is at full flower. If one wants an ineffective church club full of women and children and unrepentant homosexuals, sprinkled with emasculated men, installing a solipsistic female pastorette offers a most expeditious path. If she's married to a step-and-fetch beta boy, or attached to her lesbian lover, that's even a further improvement. If one seeks to destroy Western civilization, one couldn't do much better than to compromise the church. And so the Enemy has done, and to great effect, for he is a formidable enemy, one who would destroy us completely absent the restraint of God's strong right arm.

---

[14] National Vital Statistics Reports, Volume 61, Number 1, August 28, 2012, Table I-4.
[15] Ventura SJ., "Changing patterns of nonmarital childbearing in the United States," National Center for Health Statistics data brief, No. 18, Hyattsville, MD: National Center for Health Statistics, 2009.

For the Christian man to see clearly, his ultimate guide must be the Bible, for it has been authoritatively attested as accurate and true: In prayer to the Father, Jesus stated, "Sanctify them by the truth; *your word is truth.*"[16] Many justify their equalitarian gospel with the argument that modern culture requires us to reevaluate biblical principles, particularly those regarding sexual sin and leadership in the church. To them I ask, "Are God's precepts and instructions timeless or do they require constant evaluation based upon our space and time? Do Christians believe Elohim[17], God the Creator of time and space, bound by His own creation? Was He incapable of knowing where Western civilization would stand in the 21st century? If His clear instructions weren't timeless truths, wouldn't He have added culture-specific footnotes or qualifiers?" Either God's clear and unqualified instructions are timeless or they are not. If they are not, then we must decide which of His other instructions no longer apply because of our supposedly more advanced culture: What about his strictures regarding fornication? Sodomy? Beastiality? Murder of the unborn?

I do not jest. One can easily find churches where each of these sins is quietly tolerated, openly embraced, and even taught directly from the pulpit. Such disregard of Scripture is rebellion and arrogance on parade, reliably and demonstrably ending poorly, women and children hardest hit. I submit society's pathologies as facts in evidence of a failed feminist church: increasing dependence, rampant divorce, crashing birth rates, an utterly failed education system, routine abortion, a tsunami of out-of-wedlock births, widespread sexual sin of all types, doctors prescribing psychological medications as mere prophylactics for life's challenges, the sick and depraved entertainment culture, and ubiquitous pornography, just for

---

[16] John 17:17 (Emphasis mine.)
[17] Elohim is one of God's numerous names: God as Creator, Preserver, Transcendent, Mighty and Strong

starters. Can we at least agree that these are markers for a culture in decline? Does anyone really want to make an argument that equalitarianism and its attendant "isms" have strengthened church, culture, or country? Yes, dear reader, the Western church is compromised and the society along with it, but there is good news. Unlike many of society's ills, choosing whom to marry is a decision completely within your control, for you control the gate to commitment and it should be a narrow gate. If family is to be restored, it will be one person, one family, one church, one community at a time. Men, healing must begin in your family, with you and your decisions. If you marry, marry well.

If biblical principles are to be restored, by definition, leaders will lead the way, but, to lead well, leaders must possess integrity and develop competence. The late Stephen Covey stated it well: "Trustworthiness is more than integrity; it also connotes competence. In other words, you may be an honest doctor, but before I trust you, I want to know you're competent as well."[18] God created men to lead, but only a trustworthy man is capable of leading well in God's kingdom. Such a man must be both competent and live his life with unquestioned integrity. To possess integrity, the Christian man must authentically submit himself to God and be shaped by the Potter. To build competence, one must seek knowledge, build skills, and understand reality, seeking to understand life to the very best of one's abilities. The *Made to Lead* series is written for those men wanting the Red Pill, thirsting for Truth, wanting to lead their families and the society in which they live to a biblical understanding of life, love, obedience and sacrifice. Along with the numerous resources noted throughout, these books will greatly aid you in developing an accurate worldview and will help you better understand human nature, both critical foundations for becoming a good and godly leader. Even if your *only leadership*

---

[18] Stephen R. Covey, *Principle-Centered Leadership* (New York: Simon & Schuster, Inc., 1990), page 171.

victory in life is leading your own family well, that is a huge victory, one to be celebrated through all eternity!

With the foundation now poured, let me share to whom I wrote this book. Those who will embrace these truths at a young age will not be hindered by the adverse effects of years of bad decisions, so this information is primarily directed to young adult, single men desiring to live an impactful life; divorced men will benefit similarly. It is also written for fathers who desire to raise well-grounded sons and virtuous daughters. The married man may certainly apply these teachings to improve his own marriage. This particular book is simply too explicit for young boys, so please do not give this book to your son without reading it first. Should an authentic Christian woman elect to read this book, she would do well to start with the chapter entitled, "Raising Your Daughters." Though the subject matter covered in this book naturally taps into one's emotions, the book itself seeks to cover the material dispassionately and logically, though we'll have some fun along the way. But the equalitarian feminists, male or female, steeped in their own rhetoric, will simply wretch themselves into convulsions as they turn each page, so they read at their own risk. This book is not intended to judge, berate, or condemn; quite to the contrary, it's offered to *inform and encourage, to call men to repentance, to help them rediscover and assume their God-given responsibilities*. With that in mind, dads, please hear me, do not allow your past sins to silence your good counsel. Your children need your good and godly counsel and encouragement. Let

> ***Even if your only leadership victory in life is leading your own family well, that is a huge victory, one to be celebrated through all eternity!***

God redeem your experience, even your mistakes, to their betterment.

Please know that I have worked diligently to make this book conform to Scripture. I have brought knowledge to bear from many other sources as well, including all-important observation, often absent in the ivory tower debates. As Solomon advised, "I applied my heart to what I observed and learned a lesson from what I saw."[19] Each observation has been backtested against Scripture. If you find what you believe to be a logical or factual error, please do not hesitate to advise;[20] however, if I do not explicitly make an assertion, I have not made it, so please refrain from reflexively correcting me regarding assertions or arguments I have *not* made. Additionally, my making note of an observable tendency is not equivalent to making an unqualified assertion for all people at all times. There are always exceptions, and someone proffering a rejoinder that merely makes note of an exception to the rule does not undermine the general observation regarding the tendency. To wit, a woman successfully competing in the NBA, however unlikely that might be, would not negate the observation that men tend to be better basketball players than women.

> *...do not allow your past sins to silence your good counsel.*

I am a Christian who has "learned obedience from what he suffered,"[21] having suffered nothing in comparison to the Son, but having suffered sufficiently to understand that God uses suffering to more fully form us. God is the Potter; "we are the clay."[22] My presence on this earth means He is not done with me yet, so I likely

---

[19] Proverb 24:32
[20] The author may be contacted at Cossins@Made-to-Lead.com.
[21] Hebrews 5:8
[22] Isaiah 64:8

have more suffering ahead (as do you), but He has promised that He'll always be walking with me to and through eternity. He has been faithful. My regular prayer is that God will take my scars – those hard-earned life lessons – and use them for His redemptive purposes in many lives, in your life, just as others' scars have been redeemed in mine. May He make it so, and may any glory be His alone.

Unless you were blessed with a very wise father or grandfather or uncle, you are highly likely to have been indoctrinated into society's "isms." If this is the case, should you continue reading, I am about to challenge just about everything you've been taught your entire life, to turn it all on its head, to your and your posterity's betterment. If you are a young man without a father and without such a role model, consider letting me become that man, adopting you into sonship as you read, for reading is the purest form of listening. I do not claim perfection in any endeavor: I merely observe, think, and then act. The LORD is the creator of wisdom, but before you design to turn the next page, prepare yourself, and let history's wisest man apart from Jesus speak, "For with much wisdom comes much sorrow; the more knowledge, the more grief."[23] But in spite of the grief, the Bible tells us: "Be very careful, then, how you live – not as unwise, but as wise, making the most of every opportunity, because the days are evil."[24] "Though it cost all you have, get understanding."[25] Therefore, as a follower of Christ, it is your duty to seek wisdom and understanding: *Strap it on!*

---

[23] Ecclesiastes 1:18
[24] Ephesians 5:15
[25] Proverb 4:7

PREPARATION

Well done, good and faithful servant! You have been faithful with a few things; I will put you in charge of many things. Come and share your master's happiness![26]
— Jesus of Nazareth

If Christianity should happen to be true, then it is quite impossible for those who know this truth and those who don't should be equally well equipped for leading a good life. Knowledge of the facts must make a difference to one's actions"[27]
— C.S. Lewis

For God did not give us a spirit of timidity, but a spirit of power, of love and of self-discipline.[28]
— The Apostle Paul

---

[26] Matthew 25:21

[27] C.S. Lewis, *God in the Dock* (The Trustees of the Estate of C. S. Lewis, 1970) Part 1, Chapter 12.

[28] 2 Timothy 1:7

Moses told the Israelites: "Be strong and courageous."[29] Moses told Joshua: "Be strong and courageous."[30] God told Joshua: "Be strong and very courageous."[31] The people told Joshua, "Only be strong and courageous!"[32] Joshua told the people, "Do not be afraid; do not be discouraged. Be strong and courageous."[33] King David told Solomon: "Be strong and courageous."[34] King David tells us, "Be strong and take heart, all you who hope in the LORD."[35] Our Resurrected Lord told Paul, "Take courage!"[36] Paul tells us: "Be on your guard; stand firm in the faith; be men of courage; be strong. Do everything in love."[37]

Do you seek God's success? If so, take courage and dedicate your life to Him, to seeking His truth, to living the full life He has for you. To live such a life, live on a mission just as Paul did: let your efforts be planned and considered, but never be paralyzed for any reason. Pray, prepare, do! King Solomon wrote, "It is not good to have zeal without knowledge."[38] He didn't condemn zeal but, rather, encouraged preparation and the acquisition of knowledge as its prerequisite. Once you have obtained a base of knowledge, action will help you both refine your mind and formulate your mission.

King David wrote, "For you created my inmost being; you knit me together in my mother's womb,"[39] making it clear that God

---

[29] Deuteronomy 31:6
[30] Deuteronomy 31:7
[31] Joshua 1:7
[32] Joshua 1:18
[33] Joshua 10:25
[34] 1 Chronicles 28:20
[35] Psalm 31:23
[36] Acts 23:11
[37] 1 Corinthians 16:13
[38] Proverb 19:2
[39] Psalm 139:13

formed us with certain aspects of our character and capabilities from before birth, preparing us for our earthly mission. Our parents were tasked with nurturing what God created but, ultimately, it's up to each man to strive towards becoming all that God created him to become, to become a trustworthy man. Building competence takes enormous investments of time, so one must prepare while one can: learn, explore, read, cultivate hobbies and interests, seek counsel from parents and others whom you trust, determine what you are capable of doing and what you like doing. Read, read, read - widely and regularly. Since reading is the purest form of listening, when you read books written by wise and knowledgeable men, you will obtain knowledge distilled and recorded by history's most capable. There is no better classroom; take full advantage.

> *In formulating and executing your mission, never overlook prayer...but never let prayer excuse long-term inaction, standing idly by until God hands you life's complete script.*

Your success (and I'm speaking of life success by God's measure, not necessarily of monetary success) will be highly correlated to your effectiveness in life and effectiveness is highly correlated to mission. A man on a mission is tenacious; tenacity brings success; and success benefits you greatly: providing you quality women from whom to choose a wife; allowing you to focus resources on solving problems for yourself and others; and making you more effective as God's hands on this Earth. Take courage!

In formulating and executing your mission, never overlook prayer (as men tend to do until they're desperate), but never let prayer excuse long-term inaction, standing idly by until God hands you life's complete script. You'll still be waiting at the end of your pathetic life, hoping for eternal rewards that may never come. No, no, no, a thousand times no! Go! Do! Be a bold man of action, considered action. So long as you act within God's moral framework while seeking Him, He will bless and guide your efforts, refining you in failure and blessing you in success. He desires eternal fellowship with you starting right now, and He's the best counselor of all. If His plans differ from yours, He will let you know.

Know this well: A man who acts will outshine one who is acted upon. Harness and embrace your natural masculine energy. It's a powerful force; use it! A godly man of considered action is fearless, a leader, a good man (not a nice guy); be that man and here is what you stand to gain:

1. Praise and blessing from your God
2. Deep satisfaction and well-founded confidence that comes from preparation, toil, and success
3. Loyal friends
4. A beautiful, respectful, submissive, loving, helpful, loyal bride
5. Loving children nurtured by a wonderful, dedicated mother
6. The ability to help and counsel others in meaningful ways
7. Wisdom informed and refined by hardship, challenge, success, failure, testing, and suffering
8. An ally in eternity's God, One who will guide you, walk with you, protect you, and bring you to your eternal home with praise and rewards

Such a man just might change eternity for the better.

The effective man thinks long-term, lengthening his time preferences, a term from economics. Those who have or develop long time preferences invest current resources (time, effort, energy, money) in anticipation of long-term positive returns. To the contrary, those with short time preferences seek immediate gratification with little or no regard to long-term consequences. Those with the shortest time preferences might rob a store for a candy bar, risking the long-term pain of imprisonment for the fleeting gratification of a sweet. There are such people. My father, a now-retired state trooper, once apprehended two bank robbers who'd taken the time to stop and buy cigarettes with their loot. He let them keep them, figuring each cigarette cost them about four months in prison. Those with the longest time preferences might develop a family plan that extends for twenty generations. In general, those with longer time preferences are more productive and meet with more success over their lifetimes. God has eternal time preferences. Where are you on this continuum? Most of us should seek to lengthen our time preferences. You should find it helpful to know that men tend to have longer time preferences than women, and one would hope that Christians would develop and possess longer time preferences than their unbelieving neighbors.

> *Healthy families require intentional male leadership, and healthy families provide the foundation for healthy societies.*

In this book we will primarily examine a man's leadership role within his family, because for a family to operate as God intended, men submitted to God must lead, indeed, are commanded by God to lead. Healthy families require *intentional* male leadership, and healthy families provide the foundation for healthy societies. History reveals that societies operating absent the leadership of moral men rapidly devolve into hellish circumstances for all concerned. Both the historical record and our current circumstances warn the rational observer of our current age, and we ignore such insight at our severe peril.

Let us now forge ahead, considering a decision that will affect you and yours for eternity: whom you marry. You will find it most expedient to first understand who not to marry and why. Western women suffer greatly for their mistaken belief in feminism, as do feminist men, and they will suffer more, for a society based upon its tenants is simply unsustainable. Without great care you and your progeny will suffer too, for unlike most of her ancestral sisters, today's Western woman is conditioned and trained to reflexively rebel against male leadership, stridently recoiling from any kind of perceived control. American culture encourages her to seek happiness by walking a path virtually assured to bring her eventual sorrow and regret, affecting all those in her path and her wake. In trading the Truth for the Lie, she often ends up divorced, childless, not finding true satisfaction from her "career" but, instead, eventually finds herself alone in her fifties, lamenting with her cats the fact that her youth was misdirected to destructive or meaningless pursuits that ring hollow in later life's loneliness, well past any remedy. When one is incapable or unwilling to think things all the way through, one often ends up with precisely the opposite of one's intended goals. Pity the woman who, like Esau, has exchanged her birthright and her progeny's well-being for the proverbial bowl of stew and a piece of hardtack,[40] her family tree for the fleeting pleasure of the alpha-stimulated orgasm, suffering the excruciating pain of looking back on a wasted life. Pity her, help her, minister to her, but do not consider marrying her or her younger sister, ever.

---

[40] Genesis 25:34

Most ironically, feminism's worldly beneficiaries are not women, but certain men, promiscuous alpha males who jump from one bed to another, enjoying abundant no-cost sex with women stripped of both their clothes and their moral compass, chasing pleasure from bed to bed. For any woman seeking long-term happiness, engaging with alpha males in such behavior is not only incorrect, it is the exact opposite of correct. As I shall demonstrate, such a woman quite literally sacrifices her future marriage prospects and happiness with each new lover. If we are to save Western civilization, this dysfunctional, sinful cycle must be broken. As families are destroyed one at a time, so they must be rebuilt one at a time. To the single man, fair warning: if you marry, choose your wife carefully and well. The odds of a successful marriage in today's culture are stacked against you and today's court system stands ready, willing, and able to remove your children, take your property, and attach your future income if you choose poorly. You never, ever want to find yourself in divorce slavery, an involuntary servitude enforced by a court order, compelling you to send cash and prizes to the very woman who has destroyed your marriage and taken your children.

> **Satan seeks to exploit our appetites to our own destruction.**

One might fairly ask why the first book in a series on leadership focuses on marriage. Shouldn't a book on a man's life mission come before marriage? Yes. In a different time, marriage might be the second or even third book of this series; however, *Satan seeks to exploit our appetites to our own destruction*, and today's most widespread and most hindering mistakes in life are caving in to sexual temptation and choosing poorly in marriage. The man who marries poorly is crippled, with but little chance for him to complete a successful mission in life. As you turn the page, keep in mind that, due to her indoctrination from a young age, rare will be the modern woman who will agree with this book; however, her natural instincts will lead her to respond positively to the man who possesses such understanding.

MARRY WELL

I could never mix in the common murmur of that rising generation against monogamy, because no restriction on sex seemed so odd and unexpected as sex itself. To be allowed, like Endymion, to make love to the moon and then to complain that Jupiter kept his own moons in a harem seemed to me (bred on fairy tales like Endymion's) a vulgar anti-climax. Keeping to one woman is a small price for so much as seeing one woman. To complain that I could only be married once was like complaining that I had only been born once.[41]
— G. K. Chesterton

Any intelligent man must, at least on occasion, wonder about the meaning and purpose of his life – its trials, joys, the sweat of his brow, justice and injustice, the anxiety of life and death, the very purpose of life. Such reflection inevitably leads to searching for

---

[41] G.K. Chesterton, *Orthodoxy* (New York: Dodd, Mead & Co., 1908), page 55.

answers, for truth. The Bible contains the wisdom of the ages and its God and serves as our best source of answers to such difficult questions. But let's be completely open here: Though the Bible provides many answers, often these truths really are difficult to understand or unpack, or require context, or are buried in a bunch of "begats." Even honest scholars disagree on certain points; however and thankfully, much of the Bible's wisdom is very easy to understand once it's found. But this search takes regular effort and study, an area where busy men often fall short. (Is your head nodding in agreement?)

Think about a skill in which you're proficient. How did you master it? Complex skills are almost always developed with help from others. Several years ago I became interested in becoming a better long-range rifle shot, and, along with my fine uncle, set a goal of shooting a sub-MOA group of three shots at 1000 yards, at that distance a target about the size of a dinner plate. We began researching and found some very helpful books and articles, but, of course, the only way to shoot at 1000 yards was to actually shoot at 1000 yards. We started out at shorter ranges, working until we were sub-MOA at a particular distance and then extending the distance in 100 yard increments. Things were progressing well up to and past 700 yards, and nearly a year ago we headed up to our camp with hopes to hit our goal at the full 1000 yards. However, much to our chagrin, everything completely fell apart just past 800 yards. Not only were we not sub-MOA at 1000 yards, we weren't even consistently hitting the 4 foot by 8 foot plywood sheet backing the target. Not good. Not good at all.

Have you ever seen one of the movies depicting planes being ripped apart trying to break the sound barrier back in the forties? Transonic flight, flying at the speed of sound, presented a deadly barrier. In an attempt to break the sound barrier, Bell Aircraft was contracted to build the X-1 plane, reportedly intentionally designed with the shape of the Browning .50-caliber bullet because that bullet was known to be stable in supersonic flight. Many thought the sound barrier impenetrable by large objects until October 14, 1947 when a then-unknown Air Force pilot named Chuck Yeager passed through the barrier with the X-1 strapped to his back, christened *Glamorous Glennis* after his wife. What a story! Most surprisingly to the engineers at the time, after breaking the barrier, the plane regained its composure and flew as smoothly at supersonic speeds as at subsonic speeds. The transition was the problem, and, once the barrier was conquered, many others quickly followed in Yeager's contrails.[42]

Well, you've probably now guessed at our shooting problem. The rounds we were using exited the barrel at 2650 feet per second, well into supersonic speeds but, just past 800 yards, they went transonic and started tumbling just like those early planes - going left, right, short and just about any place other than their intended target. Even with all our ballistics charts, our chronometer, wind gauges, match-grade bullets, top-drawer optics, and careful attention paid to the smallest detail, we still had to learn by doing and, but for an old-timer that gave us a hint, we might still be wondering what went awry. We're now working on a custom load to keep the bullet supersonic past 1000 yards and will be testing it just a few weeks from this writing.[43]

The bottom line: No man will hit a target at 1000 yards without training. No matter one's natural skills, it takes serious training to master any useful skill or attain any worthy objective, and marriage is infinitely more important than punching holes in paper at 1000 yards. The wise man will give his faith (and his marriage) his considered attention in proportion to its importance.

---

[42] Chuck Yeager and Leo Janos, *Yeager* (New York: Bantam Books, 1985)
[43] I am most pleased to report that we met our goal.

Marriage is God's creation: "Has not the LORD made them one?" [44] Indeed He has and from their union, "he was seeking godly offspring."[45] Marriage is therefore where we must start, for the days demand triage. If you have married poorly, this book is not intended to condemn your previous decisions. By all means, use what you learn herein to improve your marriage, but, perhaps even more importantly, equip your children to marry well and break the cycle of dysfunction you likely inherited from your own family. Don't pass dysfunction on as an inheritance. *You must break the cycle.*

If there is any hope for a young man in Western civilization to marry well, we must be willing to engage in straight talk about what God's word reveals because the world is insane. Absolutely crazy! It's nuts to teach children how to strap a condom on a cucumber; it's crazy to provide young girls with birth control pills and abortion but many schools do, often without parental knowledge or consent; it's beyond the pale for the state of Texas to require eleven-year-old girls to be administered a dangerous vaccine to protect against a sexually transmitted disease; it's loony for parents to provide a hotel room for their daughter on prom night, pretending it's her wedding night! Our society is seriously unhinged, and we are quite literally destroying our children along with their future marriages and families through these mindless acts. Edward R. Korman, a federal judge, recently ruled that pharmacies must supply females *of any age* with the Plan B One-Step pill, a drug that terminates an early-stage pregnancy. Absurdities and contradictions abound in a failing culture, including America's: A fifteen-year-old girl can now walk into a Walgreens and buy the Plan B pill to destroy iron-clad

> ***Don't pass dysfunction on as an inheritance. You must break the cycle.***

---

[44] Malachi 2:15
[45] Ibid.

evidence of a statutory rape, her baby. Imagine this girl coming to the check-out of a California CVS with a Plan B pill, a pack of cigarettes, a sex toy, a package of condoms, and a bottle of cough medicine: "I'm sorry sweetie, but I can't sell cigarettes or cough medicine to minors. I am happy to sell you condoms, but you can get those free at school if you want to save some money. I know that Plan B pill is expensive, but I have a $10 coupon for it that will help out. By the way, that's my favorite vibrator. You'll absolutely love it." We are little different from the ancient Israelites as, "They built high places for Baal in the Valley of Ben Hinnom to sacrifice their sons and daughters to Molech."[46]

"Come out of her, my people!"[47] You do not have to partake. You don't have to sacrifice your life or your kids to Molech. *With God's help* you can carry out your mission effectively even while living in Sodom. A good and godly woman at your side is one of the most empowering weapons in any man's arsenal to accomplish God's mission. In spite of the current culture, godly and virtuous women do exist and they are waiting, hoping, and *praying* for a good, strong, godly man to love them and to lead them. I truly hope that you're praying for your future wife.

Guard against marrying the unvirtuous women, for "with her own hands the foolish [woman] tears hers down,"[48] yes, her very own house, which includes destroying her husband and children and perhaps the marriages of others in the process. "This is the way of an adulteress: She eats and wipes her mouth and says, 'I've done nothing wrong.'"[49] "A wife of noble character is her husband's crown."[50] "She is worth far more than rubies."[51] Which would you

---

[46] Jeremiah 32:35
[47] Jeremiah 51:45
[48] Proverb 14:1
[49] Proverb 30:20
[50] Proverb 12:4

prefer to marry, the woman who will become your crown or the one who will destroy you? This should not be a hard choice, but men choose poorly each and every day.

God's word commands Christians to live a life free of sexual sin. Sex is among the most powerful forces driving the actions of men. God does not hate sexual expression, not by any means. Woman, sex, marriage: it's all His wonderful creation and, expressed according to His design, sexual attraction draws men and women to marriage. Sexual expression is God's chosen means of procreation, and His plan of lifetime marriage fosters a stable society in which to raise these children. The sexual relationship also creates a powerful pair-bonding effect, one of the most important reasons that it should not be expressed outside of marriage.

God is quite clear on the rules: Women must maintain their virginity until marriage, and there is no excuse, not even if the girl gave her virginity away in the alcohol-fueled passion of prom night: "If, however, the charge is true and no proof of the girl's virginity can be found, she shall be brought to the door of her father's house and there the men of her town shall stone her to death."[52] Though we no longer stone unvirtuous women in the West, the New Testament makes it crystal clear that these Old Testament guidelines regarding sexual expression are still firmly in place. Paul wrote, "Flee from sexual immorality. All other sins a man commits are outside his body, but he who sins sexually sins against his own body."[53]

Through King Solomon, God blesses us with straight talk, and good men appreciate straight talk: "For the lips of an adulteress drip honey, and her speech is smoother than oil; but in the end she is

---

[51] Proverb 31:10
[52] Deuteronomy 22:20
[53] 1 Corinthians 6:18

bitter as gall, sharp as a double-edged sword. Her feet go down to death; her steps lead straight to the grave."[54] *She's not traveling to the grave alone if you're among her lovers* as she "multiplies the unfaithful among men."[55] Jesus takes this instruction to the next plane, from the discipline of the body to the discipline of the mind: "But I tell you that anyone who looks at a woman lustfully has already committed adultery with her in his heart."[56] Though I doubt many men (if any, beyond Jesus Himself), have followed these instructions perfectly, we must seek to stay pure, to keep our eyes away from pornographic images which feed lust, and to avoid creating such images in our own minds, "for the LORD searches every heart and understands every motive behind the thoughts."[57] Lurid fantasies feed lusts which draw us towards physical manifestations of sexual sin. Do not water the seeds of sin. Instead, seek to follow Job's good example: "I made a covenant with my eyes not to look lustfully at a girl."[58] King Solomon, who well understood the consequences of feeding and then satisfying his lusts, stated plainly: "Do not lust in your heart after her beauty or let her captivate you with her eyes, for the prostitute reduces you to a loaf of bread, and the adulteress preys upon your very life. Can a man scoop fire into this lap without his clothes being burned? Can a man walk on hot coals without his feet being scorched? So is he who sleeps with another man's wife; no one who touches her will go unpunished."[59] The Apostle Paul sums things up rather completely when he wrote: "Know ye not that the unrighteous shall not inherit the kingdom of God? Be not deceived: neither fornicators, nor idolators, nor adulterers, nor effeminate, nor abusers of themselves

---

[54] Proverb 5:3
[55] Proverb 23:28
[56] Matthew 5:28
[57] 1 Chronicles 28:9
[58] Job 31:1
[59] Proverb 6:25

with mankind…shall inherit the kingdom of God."[60] Thank God for the Savior, without whom we'd all be doomed.

Paul entreats those unable to live a virtuous single life to marry: "But since there is so much immorality, each man should have his own wife, and each woman her own husband."[61] Concerning marriage, Jesus simply and authoritatively stated, "Therefore what God has joined together, let man not separate."[62] God created male and female for His glory and sanctions their physical union within lifetime marriage. That is His plan. Engaging in sexual union outside of God's design transforms that which was meant for blessing into a bitter curse (and bitter curse is not an overstatement.) Ignore the Owner's manual at your own risk.

Outside of your decision to follow the Lord, deciding whom you marry will affect your life more than any other. The following chapters will cover the basic biblical tenants of Christian marriage and will also provide you with hard-earned and invaluable insights: first, regarding how to easily disqualify risky women; second, how to attract women of high quality; and third, encouragement and advice for those in difficult marriages.

---

[60] 1 Corinthians 6:9 (KJV)
[61] 1 Corinthians 7:1
[62] Matthew 19:6

BIBLICAL MARRIAGE

It is not good for the man to be alone. I will make a helper suitable for him.[63] — God

A hundred years ago, a mere blip in history's long march, the ideas put forth in this book regarding biblical marriage would be entirely without controversy. Then, seeing with eyes not yet fully clouded by feminism, marriage was seen as ordained by God with defined roles, men seen naturally as protectors and providers, wives as helpmeets, nurturers, and mothers. Today this taxonomy is deemed unnatural, demeaning, and even destructive. The traditional views are so far out of the zeitgeist that having authored this book recently resulted in my removal from a jury pool during voir dire. Yet, it was not always so: Dietrich Bonhoeffer was a theologian, a leader in the Confessing Church in Germany, a church opposed to Nazi interference with the church. For his opposition to Hitler, he was persecuted, imprisoned, and eventually martyred the month

---

[63] Genesis 2:18

preceding the war's end.[64] His letters from prison were assembled into a compendium and published after the war had ended. In his letters was a gift to his young niece, Renate, who married while he was in prison, a work appropriately entitled, *A Wedding Sermon from a Prison Cell.* In it, Bonhoeffer wrote the following:

> *God establishes a rule of life by which you can live together in wedlock. 'Wives, be subject to your husbands, as is fitting in the Lord. Husbands, love your wives' (Colossians 3:18-19). With your marriage you are founding a home. That needs a rule of life, and this rule of life is so important that God establishes it Himself, because without it everything would get out of joint. You may order your home as you like, except in one thing: the wife is to be subject to her husband, and the husband is to love his wife. In this way God gives to husband and wife the honor that is due to each. The wife's honor is to serve the husband, to be a 'help meet for him', as the creation story has it (Genesis 2:18); and the husband's honor is to love his wife with all his heart. He will 'leave his father and mother and be joined to his wife' (Matthew 19:5), and will 'love her as his own flesh'. A wife who wants to dominate her husband dishonors herself and him, just as a husband who does not love his wife as he should dishonors himself and her; and both dishonor the glory of God that is meant to rest on the estate of matrimony. It is an unhealthy state of affairs when the wife's ambition is to be like the husband, and the husband regards the wife merely as the plaything of his own lust for power and license; and is a sign of social disintegration when the wife's service is felt to be degrading or beneath her dignity, and when the husband who is faithful to his wife is looked on as a weakling or even a fool.*[65]

---

[64] Charles Colson, *Kingdoms in Conflict* (United States: A Judith Markman Book, 1987), page 125, provides a riveting synopsis of Bonhoeffer and the Confessing Church.
[65] Dietrich Bonhoeffer, *Letters & Papers from Prison* (New York: Touchstone, 1997), page 41.

Standing in stark contrast to Pastor Bonhoeffer's interpretation, today's feminist churchians demand "mutual submission" or "servant leadership" from their husbands which means, when boiled to its essence, the husband might lead but *only in a manner approved by his wife*, which translated to the King's English means he leads not at all. The feminist churchian seeks a puppet for a husband, with her as the puppeteer, (at least until the divorce is final when she hands the control bar to her attorney who walks it over to the judge, leaving the judge as the head of this new and exciting state-controlled relationship.) But no true leader is just a figurehead, a mere puppet. Even though Jesus sacrificed His very life for us, are we His puppeteer? Thank God, no! Good leaders are often sacrificial leaders, but they are still leaders even when leading sacrificially, perhaps especially when leading sacrificially.

It's true that both parties in a Christian marriage are to be submitted, just *not* in accordance with the feminist churchian's ideal. Their patriarchal straw man, the horrible husband, barking out orders like a two-bit dictator, concerned with only his own desires, beating his wife if his beer is insufficiently cold, doesn't even exist but in the most extreme cases, and hopefully never in the genuine Christ-follower. Feminists always drive social change by using the hard case, even when that case has to be fabricated from whole cloth, and then applying their solution for the rare or non-existent hard case to the normal case, proffering a solution for a problem that hardly exists, introducing all manner of heretofore unknown pathologies to society in the process. For example, feminists used the hard case of conception through rape to justify access to legal abortion with the full but hidden intent to make their abominable solution available in the general case, ending any pregnancy merely at the mother's whim, the father having no rights, no input whatsoever. Note well that if she decides to keep the baby, he'll be financially supporting the child until adulthood. Isn't it ironic that in the feminist's world (our world) a married woman can abort her child without her husband's consent or even his knowledge, yet many doctors will not perform a vasectomy on a married man without his wife's consent? Isn't it *his* body? Isn't it his sperm? Seek to fully comprehend the inherent dichotomy. A wife can legally abort her baby (whether fathered by her husband or not) without her husband's knowledge or consent, while the husband may find it difficult to obtain a simple vasectomy without his wife's consent.[66] The feminists seek to undermine male leadership in every area and at all cost.

The biblical model of submission is the Father leading, Christ following the Father, you following Christ, and your wife following you: "Now I want you to realize that the head of every man is Christ, and the head of the woman is man, and the head of Christ is God."[67] As hard as this might be to live out, it's not hard to understand unless one is being willingly obtuse. You follow the Lord; she follows you. You love her; she respects you: "However, each one of you also must love his wife as he loves himself, and the wife must respect her husband."[68] God will hold us responsible for how well we loved and led, just as He will hold our wives accountable for how well they respected their husbands and submitted to their leadership. God does not attach conditions to these commands, even directing Christian women to remain married to their *unbelieving* husbands.[69]

Of course, this model isn't an acceptable one to the feminist churchian, but the Bible couldn't be clearer on this topic: "Wives, submit to your husbands as to the Lord."[70] How would a feminist churchian, man or woman, react to this clear-cut passage since even

---

[66] The author is not seeking to endorse the vasectomy procedure.
[67] 1 Corinthians 11:3
[68] Ephesians 5:33
[69] 1 Corinthians 7:12
[70] Ephesians 5:22

most churchians supposedly believe the Bible to be God-breathed? It's a conundrum, a superb example of unresolved cognitive dissonance. Their equalitarian ideology precludes them from following this straightforward passage so the biblical model must be undermined at its foundation: Equality in every respect, submission in none, is the equalitarian substitute. To resolve any remaining cognitive dissonance, the churchian will predictably refer to the previous verse in Ephesians which states, "Submit to one another out of reverence for Christ"[71] and argue thusly: "Paul couldn't have really meant what he stated in verse 22 regarding marital submission since it contradicts what he wrote in verse 21. After all, even Peter wrote, '[Paul's] letters contain some things that are hard to understand.'[72] Since we find this passage hard to understand, and we know that equality is the highest virtue, we must be safe and interpret this passage as commanding husbands and wives to submit to each other." See how it's done? That's how a feminist reconciles her ideology with her faith. She alters her faith.

I suppose it's possible that the Apostle Paul, the man who authored the impeccably reasoned book of Romans, the same brilliant evangelist who reached the Greeks by seizing upon their "UNKNOWN GOD,"[73] might contradict himself from one sentence to the next. Actually, I think not: "All Scripture is God-breathed and is useful for teaching, rebuking, correcting and training in righteousness, so that the man of God may be thoroughly equipped for every good work."[74] Paul was genuinely brilliant, was blinded by Jesus on the Damascus Road,[75] was "called to be an apostle,"[76] was

---

[71] Ephesians 5:21
[72] 2 Peter 3:16
[73] Acts 17:23
[74] 2 Timothy 3:16
[75] Acts 9:1
[76] Romans 1:1

"a prisoner of Christ Jesus,"[77] literally became "an ambassador in chains,"[78] was called by God as His "chosen instrument,"[79] was a "Hebrew of Hebrews; in regard to the law, a Pharisee,"[80] and knew precisely what he was writing, expressed precisely what he meant. The fact that we now store our writings with electrons instead of scrolls doesn't invalidate Paul's clear teaching, for only a few paragraphs later he wrote: "Children, obey your parents in the Lord, for this is right."[81] Must children really obey when we've all just been instructed to submit to one another? Why? And why only a few paragraphs later would he instruct, "Slaves, obey your earthly masters with respect and fear"[82] when we're all to submit to one another? Though Peter did indeed write that Paul's letters "contain some things that are hard to understand," he continued, "which ignorant and unstable people distort, as they do the other Scriptures, to their own destruction."[83] Paul is so hard to understand, especially when one doesn't want to understand him.

Just as the adjective modifies the noun, so do the latter sentences modify the previous, starting with the general case and moving to the specific; for those readers who are computer programmers, think of it as a case statement. In general, Christians should submit to one another but Paul lays out three specific cases of emphasis: husbands and wives; parents and children; masters and slaves. Paul provided additional weight to this interpretation when he wrote that young women should be trained "to love their husbands and children, to be self-controlled and pure, to be busy at home, to be kind, and to be subject to their husbands, so that no one will malign the word of

---

[77] Philemon 1:1
[78] Ephesians 6:20
[79] Acts 9:15
[80] Philippians 3:5
[81] Ephesians 6:1
[82] Ephesians 6:5
[83] 2 Peter 3:16

God."[84] By my count, the NIV translation uses the phrase "subject to" thirty-seven times. If one peruses each instance, there is little doubt what is meant by the term, and it has nothing in common with equality or mutual submission as understood and put forth by the feminist churchian. Suffice it to say, if you're having this argument with a woman of some interest to you, I strongly advise moving along. If a woman is incapable of understanding and following God-breathed instructions written this clearly, then she is simply not a risk worth taking. There are too many worthy women in this world to settle for less. Seek the crown.

Let me be clear: God loves His people, male or female, and His earthly roles, though purposeful, are not eternal. Only God fully knows what our roles will be in heaven, but as Christians we must take great care to avoid treating others harshly or condescendingly because of their earthly gifts or roles (or lack thereof.) The Bible is filled with warnings to those who would abuse their talents or misuse their authority: "From everyone who has been given much, much will be demanded; and from the one who has been entrusted with much, much more will be asked."[85] Those tasked with leadership responsibilities must seek to execute against those responsibilities deliberately and with all care. For, when He is avenging, "It is a dreadful thing to fall into the hands of the living God,"[86] for His "judgment is just."[87] But, keeping this in mind, it is still men who are to lead. The prophet Isaiah defines disaster thusly: "As for my people, children are their oppressors, and women rule over them. O my people, they that lead thee cause thee to err, and destroy the way of thy paths."[88]

---

[84] Titus 2:4
[85] Luke 12:48
[86] Hebrews 10:31
[87] John 5:30
[88] Isaiah 3:12 (ASV)

Let's linger here for just another moment to more fully ponder a man's inherent responsibility in God's model. Jesus certainly did pick up the serving towel and wash His disciples' feet and He obviously loved His disciples unto His very death; however, He demonstrated His love by loving them enough to lead them well, whether they invited His leadership or not. Jesus didn't hesitate to use His authority to instruct, exhort, demand, or command, but He performed all of these actions in love and with consideration, *according to His Father's will*. Jesus sets a high bar, men, but His very first recorded statement to His very first disciples was a command: "Put out into deep water, and let down the nets for a catch."[89] After their nets were filled He stated, "Come, follow me, and I will make you fishers of men."[90] From His rebuke of Satan, to His command to follow, to His defiance of Pharisaic authority, to His clearing of the temple area while brandishing a whip, to His authoritative teaching and actions, to His washing of His disciples' feet, to His very death at Golgotha,[91] Jesus led perfectly, and we should follow in His path: "If you love me, you will obey what I command."[92] And note this well, even Jesus subordinates Himself to authority, God the Father: "For as the Father has life in himself, so he has granted the Son to have life in himself. And he has given him authority to judge because he is the Son of Man."[93] Anyone who designs an organization with no clear line of authority is a fool, and God is no fool. He's God, by definition the antithesis of a fool. Even Heaven itself has clear lines of authority. Churches do too, especially, and most ironically, in those churches advocating equalitarianism in marriage. Stir the pot in an equalitarian congregation, and you'll quickly see those lines emerge in deep

---

[89] Luke 5:4
[90] Matthew 4:18
[91] Matthew 27:32
[92] John 14:15
[93] John 5:26

relief. The family is also an organization and requires clear leadership too. You are called and commanded to provide it.

Where can one find a wife who will become a crown? How can one identify a woman who'd make a loving, respectful, submissive wife, a woman willing to join you in your mission, separating her from the morass of her rebellious sisters? Once you've sufficiently prepared, the next step is simple really, for you must meet her to evaluate her: Follow Jesus' model with His disciples and take charge from the very moment you meet. If you're interested, don't timidly ask her out. Tell her you find her interesting, that you'd like to see her on Friday, and that you'll pick her up at seven. If she reacts in the negative, just pass, and celebrate that you've probably saved yourself time, effort, and energy towards a dead-end. After all, time and resources are limited and there are plenty of girls available for the man on a mission. This is truth men: Though the percentage of virtuous women has decreased, there are still millions of good women available for the capable, courageous man.

> ***Countless potentially good marriages have been lost before they began through a man's timidity and his fear of rejection.***

Take courage, men. Countless potentially good marriages have been lost before they began through a man's timidity and his fear of rejection. Have you ever noticed or wondered why good salesmen are often married to exceptionally pretty women? Their professional life is full of rejection and they must overcome their prospect's objections repeatedly to be successful. They understand that selling is a game of large numbers, that if only one percent of people need their product, they are going to have to be rejected ninety-nine times for every sale. If a salesman can't deal with rejection routinely, he's in the wrong business, and will have to find other employment. So what are you afraid of? Is that five foot, two inch, one hundred and fifteen pound girl going to put you in the emergency room with her strong right punch? Is her rejection going to ruin your life? No and no. You should work to become fearless around women, to disregard their beauty when interacting with them; she's not remotely capable of injuring you during your waking hours; if you get rejected ten thousand times and then meet your perfect wife, you are a winner. In marriage, you only have to make the successful sale one time! Put in its proper perspective, rejection really is not a big deal; after all, who should you fear, God or woman? Truly you must decide, "Do I fear woman?" Men who are successful with women don't fear them, or at least find ways to overcome their fear.

You can be certain of this: If you fail to muster the courage to approach a woman of interest, you certainly won't be able to lead her in lifetime marriage. Even more importantly, how will such a man bear up under adversity or persecution when it comes? Seriously, be about your business. Take courage. Let the memory of your fearless approach marinate for a lifetime in her mind. Courage is attractive. College, the grocery, sporting events, the cafeteria – girls are where you find them. Think. Man up. Invite her in.

Harvey Mackay gives great business advice and his "Rule of Ten Thousand" is very applicable to this problem:

When you were a kid, you wouldn't get the pie unless you ate the peas. As we get older, it gets more sophisticated. They don't threaten to fire you to get a day's work out of you.

But there is a variation of the peas/pie gambit that still gets results. One of the country's most successful college basketball coaches uses the Rule of Ten Thousand. Or rather, ten thousand dollars.

"You miss more free throws than any other starter on this team," he says. "You say you can't make free throws?"

"Now, what if I were to pay you ten thousand dollars to shoot above the league average in free throws the rest of the season? Could you hit sixty-five percent?"

"Yeah, I know I can."

"Yeah, I know you can, too. Only there's just one thing. I'm not going to pay you ten thousand dollars. You are going up to that line, and every time you shoot I want you to think you're shooting for that ten thousand dollars."

A 50 percent free-throw shooter became a 70 percent shooter, for a coach whose teams appeared in the NCAA tournament more often than any other team in his region.[94]

Could you muster the courage to approach a woman of interest if someone paid you ten thousand dollars to do so? Of course you could. (If not, just stop reading now and resume your favorite video game. Being single has its advantages.)

Let us take this idea a step further: I once employed a wonderful woman as my office manager, a woman who joined the company in its infancy and contributed to its success for many years. When something needed to be done, I could hand it off to her and know that nothing would keep her from accomplishing the goal. She stunned me with her tenacity repeatedly. If a task was possible to

---

[94] Harvey Mackay, *Beware the Naked Man Who Offers You His Shirt* (New York: William Morrow and Company, Inc., 1990), page 40.

accomplish, it would be done. She was indispensable, a lioness, and she was compensated accordingly. Interestingly though, in her personal life she was precisely the opposite, so considerate and intent on not inconveniencing another soul on this earth that she lived less than the full life that was before her. Every day, the moment she left the office, the lioness transformed into the lamb. Eventually we became close enough for me to inquire directly about my observation and she answered candidly, "You are paying me to get a job done and that makes it my responsibility to get it done." Though hers was a stunning transformation, I've since noted that many men also behave similarly, a tiger at work, castrated for the remaining hours in the day. A man castrated for half his waking hours cannot become all that God would have him to become, so I have a suggestion for your consideration: As a Christian, you are in God's army 24/7, and are more accountable to Him than to any employer or customer. If you are capable of knocking down walls for a paycheck, can't you embrace your masculinity sufficiently to knock down walls for the God of the Universe, your Creator? Can't you knock down walls to marry well and thereby bless yourself and your children with a good marriage? Can't you knock down a few walls to enjoy sex often with your lovely wife? Yes you can, and it will both please your God and benefit you greatly. To the point, to successfully find (and marry) a virtuous wife in Sodom, you will need your chest, so don't leave it hanging in the closet my brother. Your future children are depending upon your ability to marry well.

Though God commands wives to respect their husbands, the wise husband will seek to engender respect, to become a man worthy of respect. The man too timid to approach a woman of interest will not command any woman's respect but "the righteous are as bold as a lion."[95] Don't you seek His righteousness? Be courageous. Be bold. Be a lion.

---

[95] Proverb 28:1

AVOIDING THE SCOURGE OF DIVORCE

I love divorce.[96] — Satan

I was sitting at lunch with Jeren as he held back tears, recounting how his wife, Laura, had connected with Bill via Facebook, an old high school flame, and was now meeting him at nightclubs. She'd stayed out all night the night before, not for the first time, but claimed, "Nothing had happened except a kiss." Translation: "Bill is exciting! I'm really attracted to him and I've had wild sex with him several times. He's not boring like Jeren, but I'm not sure yet whether or not Bill will commit to me, so I have to keep Jeren from bolting until I'm ready to dump him. But he knows that something is up, so I'd better admit to indiscretions too small for him to jettison our marriage but sufficient to seem plausible. I'll tell him I need some space and that we might still have a chance with some counseling. Hmmm. I think he'll go for it! The dupe." Having seen

---

[96] In Malachi 2:16, God states, "I hate divorce." I believe it logically follows that Satan must love it.

this scenario play out any number of times, the pattern of behavior is utterly predictable.

Jeren is the classic nice guy who happens to be a very handsome man, a genuine Christian, a very good provider, a loyal friend and husband, the best man Laura will ever entice to marriage. He loves his kids well and is a man you'd be happy to have your daughter marry. So what in the world was his wife thinking, putting her entire marriage at risk for a high-risk fling? Though the reasons are usually manifold and are never an excuse for sin, the overriding problem was that she no longer respected Jeren and when respect wanes, so does attraction. In addition, she'd also surrounded herself with divorcées, hearing all about the joys of being newly single. After all, once a decision is made, it's only natural to justify it. "Bad company corrupts good character."[97]

Jeren, completely caught off guard as nice guys often are, reacted as most men do in this situation, precisely the opposite of that which might save his marriage: he tearfully begged her to stay, promised to change diapers and wash half the dishes if only she'd *please* stay. He told her that he was willing to change, to make things better, and didn't want to lose her. Imagine what this tearful exchange did for any remaining vestiges of respect she might have held for her husband. Poof! Gone!

After listening to him for some time and asking many questions, I gave Jeren (and have given many other Nice Guy Jerens) this advice: "Get angry and go home. Tell your wife that you love her and that you want to save your marriage, but inform her that her nightclub days are over as of this moment and that if she ever has the least dalliance with another man that the marriage is over, kaput, done, and it'll be the nastiest divorce she could possibly imagine.

---

[97] 1 Corinthians 15:33

Then take her phone, call this Bill derelict, and inform him that if he so much as texts your wife in the future, you'll track him down like a junkyard dog."

He recoiled and informed me that she'd immediately leave for her friends, to which I responded, "So what, Jeren? She's all but declared your marriage over. A kiss? She's probably sleeping with him, dude! Hello! Is she sleeping with you? Has she slept with you in six months? Hello! Your marriage is broken. Your only hope is to reestablish her respect for you and fast. To do so you're going to have to be a little crazy, a bit out-of-control – no more tears, no more begging, just raw, manly, testosterone-laden leadership. If she leaves, then the moment she leaves, start hauling her stuff out to the front yard, preferably while she's still backing out of the driveway – clothes, jewelry, books, everything that's hers."

> *Women possess an innate desire to control their man but don't respect a man they can control.*

You, dear reader, may think my advice over-the-top, but they survived Jeren's reset and, last we spoke, they were still married and working on their new relationship, Jeren leading the way, his children living in an intact home, his wife both respecting and attracted to her newfound alpha man. What woman couldn't rest easy in the arms of such a man? *Women possess an innate desire to control their man but don't respect a man they can control.* Though this appears to be a contradiction on its face, it actually makes perfect sense. Women naturally seek security, and a man who can be controlled is likely not a good protector. His independence serves as a proxy for his strength.

Heed the warning in Jeren's story: Given the feminist, divorce-centric culture we find ourselves in, you must marry well or you risk becoming a literal divorce slave to an ex-wife through no choice of your own. Jeren's only possible path to save his marriage was in reassuming the leadership role that he'd been unwittingly abdicating for so long. Thankfully, Laura elected to stay, but divorce slavery is a true risk for any married man. *Your wife can divorce you at any time, for any reason, or for no reason at all.*

> *Your wife can divorce you at any time, for any reason, or for no reason at all.*

I once found myself on a lunch date on Kansas City's Country Club Plaza with a striking young woman of twenty-five who, come to find out, had been divorced the year before. I began asking her the reasons behind her divorce and she stated, "Well, my husband relocated to continue his education, and we just sort of drifted apart." No kidding? Who could have possibly anticipated that a young married couple living across the state from one another might drift apart? When I asked why she hadn't relocated to join her husband, she replied that she just really liked Kansas City and didn't want to leave. Unbelievable. What a frivolous divorce. I'll bet her former husband didn't realize that her marriage vows only applied within the city limits of Kansas City. He chose poorly. Suffice it to say, that lunch was both our first and last date.

If your wife files for divorce without any cause, it has no bearing on the court's decisions. In fact, the government will likely assist her with all manner of financial aid to enable her departure. Even as I write these very words, a man with whom I've been walking for over a year is in conference with his wife and their lawyers, arguing and dividing up the human and material possessions of their twenty year marriage, a divorce that he completely opposes. In this case, as in many others, her fellow churchians and the Federal government have come alongside to enable her unbiblical choices.

If you find yourself in similar circumstances and you have children, she will almost assuredly secure custody and, via the courts, force you into divorce slavery while she likely sleeps with a series of increasingly questionable men, their quality decreasing in proportion to her partner count, the entire process utterly destroying your children. Think about this: It's highly likely that she'll be paying for her transient lover's dinner with your child support payments! Perhaps most seriously of all, sexual abuse of daughters at the hands of the ex-wife's lovers or her new husband is legion: "One study found that a preschooler living with a stepfather was *forty times* more likely to be sexually abused than one living with both of his or her biological parents."[98]

Antony was a 3rd century Christian whom God led to a life of self-denial. Some consider him the first monk. His ministry was fruitful, drawing explicit attack from the Enemy. In one such attack, the devil tempted him as he "took upon him the shape of a woman and imitated all her acts simply to beguile Antony." But Antony, though tempted, "turned his thoughts to the threatened fire and the gnawing worm" and "passed through the temptation unscathed."[99] In like manner, let the nightmarish thought of divorce and its horrible aftermath spur you to the effort and discipline required to attract and marry a virtuous woman, a woman who will become your crown, a woman who will "bring [you] good, not harm, all the days of her life."[100] Such a woman will never consider divorce, a problem much

---

[98] W. Bradford Wilcox et al., *Why Marriage Matters: Twenty-Six Conclusions from the Social Sciences, Second Edition* (New York: Institute for American Values, 2005), page 32.
[99] *The Life of St. Antony*, an ancient work often credited to Athanasian, page 198.
[100] Proverb 31:12

easier avoided than rectified or endured. Then lead your family well, every single day that God gives you breath.

Given today's culture there is absolutely no reason for a man to be swayed by pressure to marry for it is *far, far better* to not marry than to marry poorly. Do you still think I exaggerate marital risk? With approximately half of all marriages ending in divorce, the United States has among the highest divorce rates in the entire world. Though the statistics vary somewhat, on average first marriages have between a forty to fifty percent chance of ending in divorce, while divorce rates for subsequent marriages are significantly higher.[101] The various studies, literature, and statistics all agree that *women initiate divorce significantly more often than men.* According to one survey-based study, sixty-six percent of women stated that they instigated their divorce.[102] So with up to fifty percent of first marriages ending in divorce and two-thirds of divorces being initiated by women, statistically you have a one in three chance of that lovely creature you have every intention of loving for life inviting you via court summons to a much different relationship: divorce slavery. In a separate study of divorced people, it was determined that the woman was more than three times more likely to indicate that she wanted a divorce while her husband did not, than to indicate that her husband wanted a divorce but that she did not.[103] This is a monumental disparity. Modern marriage is no longer considered a lifetime vow, but merely a civil contract that

---

[101] Jennifer Baker of the Forest Institute of Professional Psychology in Springfield, Missouri, has been widely quoted as stating, "Fifty percent of first marriages, sixty-seven percent of second marriages and seventy-four percent of third marriages end in divorce." The motivated reader can search census data, any number of surveys, and numerous academic articles for more detailed information.

[102] Xenia Montenegro et al., "The Divorce Experience: A Study of Divorce at Midlife and Beyond," *AARP The Magazine*, May 2004.

[103] Margaret F. Brinig and Douglas W. Allen, "These Boots Are Made for Walking: Why Most Divorce Filers Are Women," *American Law and Economics Review*, 2000, volume 2, pages 126-169.

your wife can break at will, her relinquishing all of her marital responsibilities to you, while using the court's power to keep your financial responsibilities substantially in place, sometimes for more than twenty years via child support and, possibly, maintenance payments. In summary, if she seeks a divorce, you have no legal remedy to prevent it, and a woman is much more likely to seek divorce than her husband.

To a thinking man, such statistics might properly dissuade him from seeking marriage at all. Certainly, if a man has no moral qualms with sexual relationships outside of marriage, becoming a sexually active single may well be the short-term pleasurable path in today's culture, but the Christian man desiring sexual expression and a family must either marry or live outside his faith. The horrid statistics should not dissuade him from marriage, merely make him *extremely* careful in his selection process, for marriage to an authentic Christian woman is one of life's greatest blessings. The adjective "authentic" being the key: W. Bradford Wilcox asserts that the more serious a couple is about their faith, the lower the likelihood of divorce. He contends that a nominal Protestant's risk of divorce is higher than the national average by twenty percent, while a conservative Protestant's is lower by ten percent, and an active conservative Protestant's is lower by thirty-five percent.[104]

I would contend that choosing very carefully all but eliminates the risk of divorce; therefore, a Christian man should step into marriage without fear, but he should avoid taking such momentous steps without thought, care, prayer, and counsel. In fact, it is a good practice, and the Bible provides a number of examples, of His followers fasting and praying for the Lord's guidance regarding

---

[104] W. Bradford Wilcox and Elizabeth Williamson, "The Cultural Contradictions of Mainline Family Ideology and Practice," in *American Religions and the Family*, ed. Don S. Browning and David A. Clairmont (New York: Columbia University Press, 2007), page 50.

important decisions or events. Relying on reason alone to make decisions makes for poor decisions, for our minds are fallible and we're always operating with incomplete information. Just as the Hivites tricked Joshua into making a treaty with them against God's instructions because they "sampled their provisions," but failed to "inquire of the LORD,"[105] too many men choose to make crucial decisions in ignorance and vacuum, to their great detriment, for the statistics do not lie. When one is living in a feminist culture, approaching marriage seriously and prayerfully is a prerequisite for completing a meaningful mission in life. By its very definition, divorce destroys marriage, but its virulent wake is far wider, harming your mission and devastating your children for the remainder of their lives, often passing the dysfunction on to the next generation. According to the white paper, *Second Chances*:

We now know that divorce on average has dramatic effects on children's lives, across the life course. Research shows that divorced fathers and mothers are less likely to have high-quality relationships with their children. Children with divorced or unmarried parents are more likely to be poor, while married couples on average build more wealth than those who are not married, even accounting for the observation that well-off people are more likely to get married. Parental divorce or failure to marry appears to increase children's risk of failure in school. Such children are less likely to finish high school, complete college, or attain high-status jobs. Infant mortality is higher among children whose parents do not get or stay married, and such children on average have poorer physical health compared to their peers with married parents. Teens from divorced families are more likely to abuse drugs or alcohol, get in trouble with the law, and experience a teen pregnancy. Numerous studies also document that children living in homes with unrelated men are at much higher risk of childhood physical or sexual abuse. These

---

[105] Joshua 9:11

studies generally adjust for parental education and income, which means that the negative effects cannot be explained by these demographic factors.[106]

Just as bad habits are hard to break, so too are injurious cycles once ingrained in a society or family. Once divorce enters a family tree, it establishes a cycle that is near impossible to break. This same paper cited research that concludes a parental divorce increases the chance of a child from that marriage divorcing *by at least fifty percent* over a child from an intact family! Further, it found that a child of divorce was fifty percent more likely to marry another child of divorce and marriages formed under those circumstances were *three times more likely* to divorce than marriages of children where both were raised in intact families.[107]

> **When a woman tells you she's divorcing her husband "for the good of the children," it's good and proper to treat her claim with deep skepticism.**

A separate and informative eight-decade long study found that parental divorce actually shortened the lifespans of the effected children: "Children from divorced families died almost five years earlier on average than children from intact families. Parental divorce, not parental death, was the risk factor. In fact, parental divorce during childhood was the *single strongest social predictor*

---

[106] William J. Doherty and Leah Ward Sears, *Second Chances – A Proposal to Reduce Unnecessary Divorce* (New York: Institute for American Values, 2011).
[107] Ibid.

(emphasis mine) of early death, many years into the future."[108] When a woman tells you she's divorcing her husband "for the good of the children," it's good and proper to treat her claim with deep skepticism.

Ponder these statistics. Understand them. Let them guide you and choose carefully whom you marry. I'm not suggesting that you not consider marrying a woman from a broken home without due regard for other items of importance (after all, her parent's divorce wasn't her fault); however, do so knowing that her parent's divorce will impact you and your marriage in significant ways. Detached observation, pattern matching, prayerful inquiry, seeking trusted outside counsel, and thoughtful analysis provide the intelligent man tools with which to make good decisions. Ignore them at your peril.

> *Finally, as you ponder a marital decision with a mind addled and impaired by sexual desire, keep in mind that your ex-wife won't be having sex with you and, as a Christian, your options for sex without sin will be gone along with your kids, half your wealth, and a sizable portion of your future earnings.*

Never forget that you are under no obligation to marry until you're married. Yes, that's a simple statement, but do not laugh. Men have been "forced" into marriage through threats of suicide. Live free!

Finally, as you ponder a marital decision with a mind addled and impaired by sexual desire, keep in mind that *your ex-wife won't be*

---

[108] Howard S. Friedman and Leslie R. Martin, *Surprising Discoveries for Health and Long Life from the Landmark Eight-Decade Study* (New York: Hudson Street Press, 2011), page 80.

having sexual relations with you and, as a Christian, your options for sex without sin will be gone along with your kids, half your wealth, and a sizable portion of your future earnings. If you marry, marry well.

SEXUAL MARKET VALUE

But judgments of value are necessarily always personal and subjective.[109]
— Ludwig von Mises

At its root economics is simply a study in human action so it should not be surprising when its findings are widely applicable in areas normally considered as outside of pure economic analysis. The law of supply and demand is a simple and extremely useful example. In an unfettered economy, the economic law of supply and demand states that a product's price will adjust until the supply meets the demand, that price known as the market clearing price. It then logically holds that as supply increases in relation to demand, the market clearing price will decrease. Conversely, as demand increases relative to supply, the market clearing price will rise. In the simple graph below, the market clearing price is five dollars. An

---

[109] Ludwig von Mises, *Profit and Loss* (Auburn, Alabama: Ludwig von Mises Institute, 2008), page 18, based upon a paper written in 1951.

understanding of this straightforward economic law will provide the perceptive man insights into many areas of life.

Within the socio-sexual marketplace, men and women assign values to each person as well, a value that could be considered as a sexual market value, or SMV for short. Think of SMV as a price, one that is negotiated between a potential buyer and a potential seller and is firmly established upon an agreement to sell (or rent, as the case may be.) A person's SMV is always determined by the opposite sex and is a composite of all the factors that would increase or decrease a person's sexual attractiveness. Just as with any product, how the various factors are considered and weighed will vary from person to person, for value is always subjective. Think of your SMV as money in your pocket. To a woman considering marriage, your SMV in her eyes must be sufficient for the "purchase" or her answer will be no. SMV is subject to change and the thinking man will endeavor to maximize and maintain his SMV over time, both before and after the marriage vows are made.

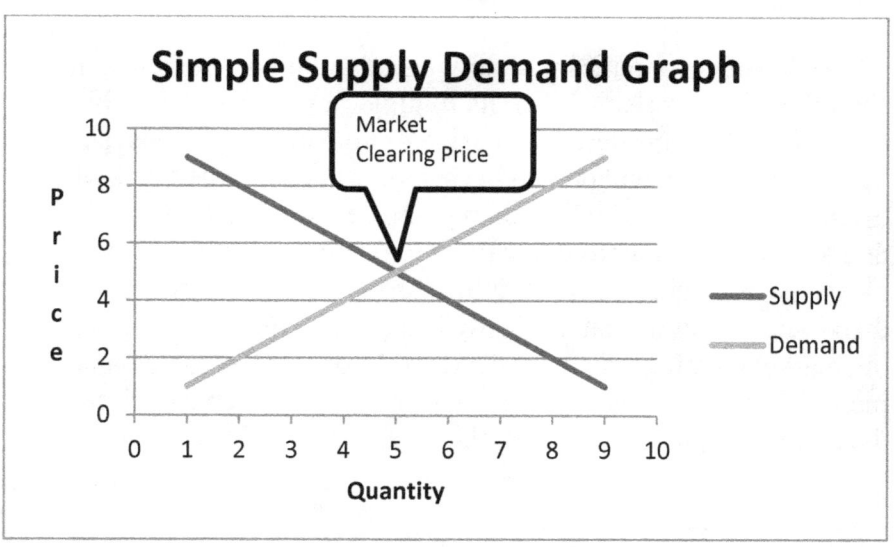

Just like the price of a Ferrari or a bushel of wheat, the SMV price calculation is subjective, near infinitely complex, and is notably affected by supply and demand. For example, if you were to visit the Missouri Institute of Science and Technology in Rolla, a quality engineering school located in a relatively isolated town with a student body comprised of four men to every woman, you would see the law of supply and demand in action. Demand for women far outstrips supply, and you'll routinely find high SMV men attached to women with a much lower SMV. I certainly wouldn't want to raise a rebellious daughter in Rolla, being female there roughly the equivalent of being water to a man dying of thirst. Applying the law of supply and demand to his situation, the observant male Rolla student might consider moving to Tuscaloosa upon his graduation.

A woman's physical beauty, the primary determinant of her SMV, is at its peak from the age of seventeen to about twenty-five and begins to wane rapidly after the age of thirty-five. A woman's fertility peak coincides almost perfectly with her peak SMV. (Funny how that works.) The chart below plots a hypothetical high value woman's SMV (we shall name her Cheerleader) against the average woman's fertility over that same time period, as measured by the probability of conception with regular unprotected sexual activity.[110] A woman aged twenty to twenty-four has an eighty-six percent probability of conceiving over time. Ten years later that same woman has a sixty-three percent chance of conceiving and ten years after that only a thirty-six percent probability of conceiving. A woman aged forty-five to forty-nine has only a one in twenty chance of conceiving a child. If you want a large family, marry a young woman.

---

[110] Helen Nelson Carcio, *Management of the Infertile Woman* (Philadelphia, Pennsylvania: Lippincott Williams & Wilkins, 1998), chart effects smoothed.

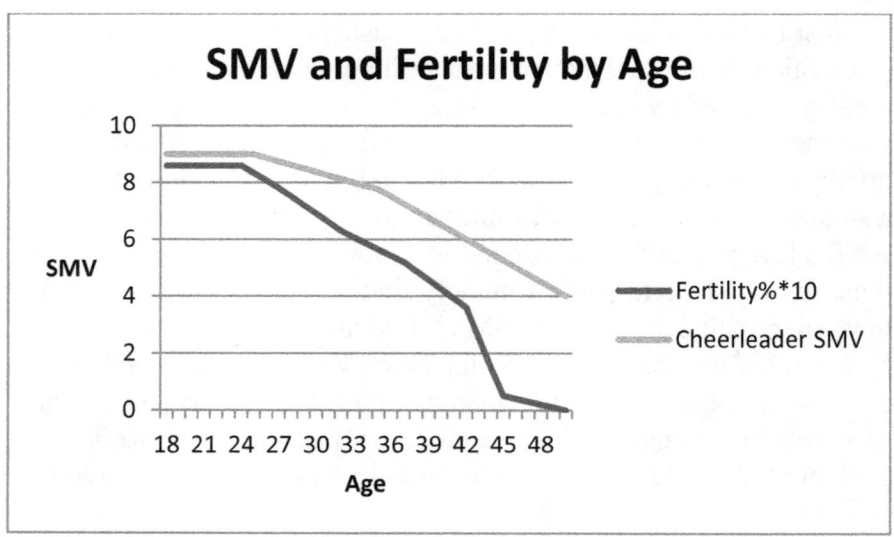

Think of the difference in female and male SMV like this: An eighteen-year-old woman is like a shiny new car, beautiful, but destined to depreciate based upon the years, how well it's maintained, and how hard it's driven. Wrecking the car severely reduces its value instantaneously. The eighteen-year-old man is more akin to a vintage 'Cuda, complete, original, but stored in a barn and in poor condition. The barn-find 'Cuda has some standing value which varies depending upon several factors: the engine with which it's equipped (gotta go with the Hemi), if it's original, if it's numbers matching, if it comes with the original build sheet, and other options with which it's equipped. But its true value lies in its *potential* which will require a lot of time, effort, and energy to bring to concours condition. When it comes to SMV, women are born more than made and men are made more than born.

Though a man's SMV is influenced by his looks, particularly for younger men, not nearly to the same extent as for women, his SMV being more highly correlated to his social status and his resources (or his apparent potential to secure future resources.) A capable man's SMV peak comes at least ten years later than a woman's, often in his mid to late-thirties, a decade or more after his absolute physical peak. The more successful the man, the longer his SMV remains high. Do not miss this vital contrast: After the age of forty, a woman is virtually invisible in the sexual marketplace compared to her relative position when she was twenty-five while a successful man is at or just past his all-time SMV peak.

> *Do not miss this vital contrast: After the age of forty, a woman is virtually invisible in the sexual marketplace compared to her relative position when she was twenty-five while a successful man is at or just past his all-time SMV peak.*

The graph below illustrates this observation by graphing the SMV by age of our Cheerleader along with a hypothetical man, the Quarterback, both possessing a very high peak SMV, but the pattern is just as pertinent to a matched couple with lower SMV peaks. For the purposes of this discussion, as in real life, it's important to note that this chart represents the person's SMV as it would be rated by the opposite sex when the opposite sex is at his or her peak SMV. Note that within this hypothetical couple their relative sexual market value meets at about the age of twenty-nine, as the man's SMV is increasing and the woman's is beginning to decrease. After they each reach the age of about thirty-eight, the man will hold a relative SMV three full points higher than the woman, a differential that might be maintained for decades, even though their respective SMV peaks were close to identical.

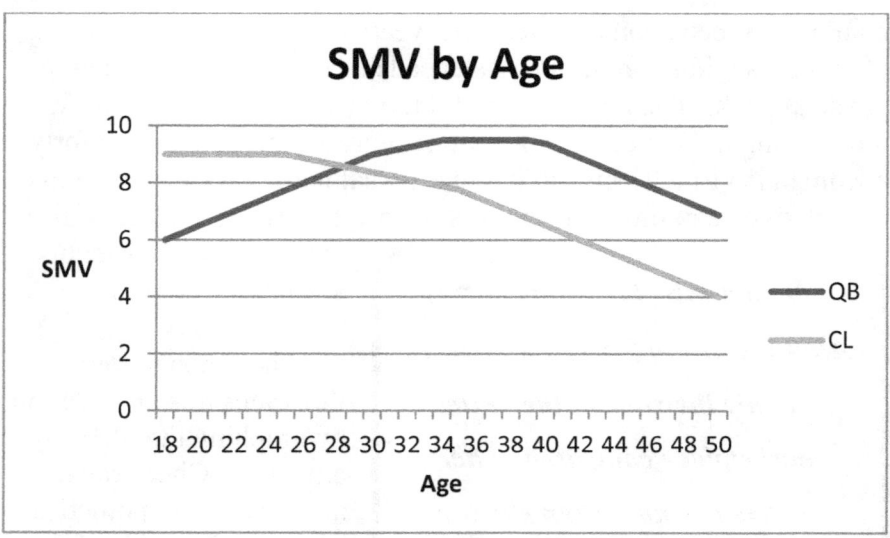

This observation has implications for the man who seeks to marry well. When does a professional athlete want to be negotiating his compensation package? Of course, he hopes that his contract expires just after a spectacular season, hopefully one in which he's been a post-season star, being named the MVP of the championship team the practical equivalent to owning his own bank. Joe Flacco is living that dream as of this writing, having been named MVP of Superbowl XLVII and becoming a free agent at the end of that very game. Perfect. Be like Joe.[111]

The best time to negotiate anything is when one possesses maximum leverage or value and marriage is no different. To attract the highest quality woman, it behooves a man to stay single until he's approaching his SMV peak, when his "currency" is highest, waiting until at least his late twenties to consider marriage. The moral Christian man's initial response to this advice will likely be:

---

[111] For the record, Joe did score a big contract a month after his Super Bowl victory, history's most lucrative NFL player contract at over $20 million dollars per year for the next six years. Nice.

"Cossins, you can't serious. I will die of sexual starvation before I hit maximum SMV." While each man's sexual appetite will influence his decisions (just part of the total marriage calculus), as in all areas of life, some men will have longer time preferences, content to delay the benefits of marriage in order to secure a high quality woman five to ten years his junior when he's thirty-four, while others will have shorter time preferences and will marry a woman much closer to his own age while he's in his early twenties. It's no sin either way, merely preference. Just keep in mind that Christian marriage is a *lifetime* vow, one that you'll be better able to negotiate the closer you are to your peak SMV. The man with longer time preferences will generally marry better.

Don't miss the important corollary here: A woman should seek to marry at the peak of her SMV as well, seeking marriage at a young age to a good man with lots of potential who's three or more years her senior. The graph below plots the SMV curves for the same two people but adjusted for the Cheerleader being five years younger than the Quarterback. There are many benefits to such an age disparity in marriage: By marrying a more tested and established man she will generally find it easier to genuinely respect him. Examine her adjusted lifetime SMV curve and you'll see that it tracks more closely to her husband's than the same-age couple above, helping to reduce his temptations in mid-life since the wider the gap in a couple's SMV, the higher the temptation.[112] Additionally, with a significant age disparity, his SMV will be peaking as she traverses her peak SMV period, the time of highest divorce risk for women.[113] Considering these latter two points

---

[112] General Patraeus' recent affair with his biographer, twenty years his junior, is a good example. Though in his sixties and no handsome man, his status kept his SMV high while his same-aged wife looked positively grandmotherly in comparison to his illicit lover.

[113] S. L. Brown et al, "Age Variation in the Divorce Rate, 1990-2010," National Center for Family and Marriage Research, 2012.

together, one can logically conclude that an age difference will mitigate the risks of moral failure by either party. With this five year age disparity, both will likely marry closer to their SMV peak and the maximum SMV delta is decreased by nearly half in relation to a same-age marriage throughout the period of their highest divorce risk.

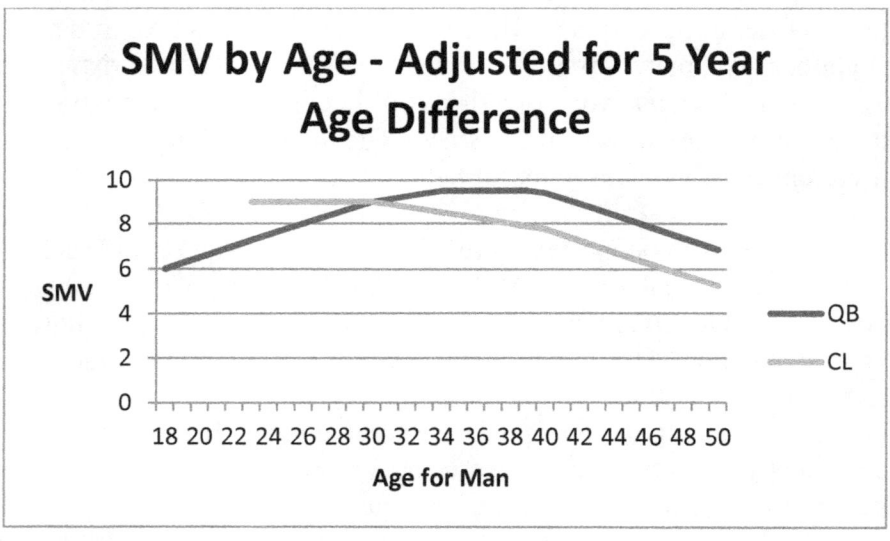

Though a woman's SMV peaks on or before her mid-twenties, during the beginning phase of the decline it will not have a noticeable effect on male interest; however, every woman comes with a marriage expiration date (MED), past which it's highly unlikely that she'll be able to marry a quality, never-married man within five years of her own age.[114] For example, in the calendar year of 2005, the state of Michigan recorded that the highest number of first marriages for men took place in the age group of twenty-five to twenty-nine. This is not surprising, but take note that the age

---

[114] 2005 Michigan Occurrence Marriage Files from the Michigan Vital Records and Health Data Development Section.

group of thirty to thirty-four had fewer than one-half the number of first marriages as the previous age group, with the next older five year grouping halving that number yet again. Though many men are marrying in their thirties, there are a decreasing number of first marriages and an increasing number of second marriages; therefore, for the vast majority of women, that all-important marriage expiration date is just two years past thirty. Her thirtieth birthday is a bad day for the unattached and unmarried woman who desires legitimate children of her own making. For many women the approach of MED might be the first warning knock of reality upon the feminist's fantasy world.

After all, even chasing that elusive feminist dream, most women still pine for their McMansion and the obligatory two children, one of each please, boy first if at all possible. Warning: As a woman approaches and passes her marriage expiration date, she will become increasingly desperate and will begin considering settling (and that's what it generally is) for a provider man to whom she probably wouldn't have given the time of day when she was at her SMV peak and the center of male attention. I am not recommending that you disqualify out-of-hand a woman who's approaching her MED. It's merely one more consideration to add to your marriage calculus, but consider the situation carefully. You do not want to marry a woman who is merely settling, as her chance of experiencing post-marital buyer's remorse is high, increasing your chance of divorce slavery.

Having made these good and honest observations regarding the dynamics of sexual market value, I trust that it's perfectly obvious that each man will assign differing values to different characteristics in forming their own judgments. In this chapter, I've dealt primarily with SMV dynamics, not with how any man might judge the attractiveness of a particular woman for marriage, but pretty, sweet, shapely, demure, and trim never goes out of style.

HYPERGAMY

The first two facts which a healthy boy or girl feels about sex are these: first that it is beautiful and then that it is dangerous.[115]
— G. K. Chesterton

In this journey you will find it most helpful to understand the meaning of a word you've likely never heard: hypergamy. Female hypergamy is the strong desire for a woman to attach herself to the highest value man she can attain. Women have been hypergamous throughout all of history (understandably so), and so it follows that God created woman with a hypergamous nature. Female hypergamy isn't good or bad in and of itself but, depending upon the surrounding culture, it can serve to either strengthen or weaken marriage, both individually and the very institution itself. Let me explain.

---

[115] G. K. Chesterton, *Illustrated London News,* January 9, 1909.

In a culture of high sexual restraint (HSR), hypergamy strengthens marriage as virginal women will tend to marry early to the best man they can attract into a faithful, fruitful, and long-term marriage. Sexual restraint encourages earlier marriage because that is the path to sexual expression and men, especially, are extremely driven to women by their sexual urges. (Never apologize; it's how we're wired.) When women at large deny premarital sex, men commit to marriage as a matter of course. As the gatekeeper to sex, the intelligent woman will use a man's sexual appetite to draw him to commitment. When marriage is the path to sexual release, men will focus their pursuits on women with whom they might consider marriage, thereby keeping women realistic in what man they might possibly obtain marital commitment, the homely woman not confusing herself with the comely, the Quarterback hardly acknowledging the homely girl's existence. In the HSR culture the Quarterback will marry the virginal Cheerleader and Steady Sam, the town's best Ford mechanic, will marry Homely Harriett, also a virgin, as chastity is highly valued. Both new families will prosper to their own degree, will have and raise children, and will remain married for life.

The HSR culture encourages fidelity and, just as importantly, provides strong disincentives to those women who stray. Such societies tend to have earlier marriage, more and healthier children and, without cultural disruption, tend to nurture a healthy and stable society with higher rates of marriage, fewer divorces, and a higher percentage of the adult population enjoying sexual relationships. Such are the markers for a productive, stable, long-lived culture. Such was the culture of America prior to the Progressivism of the early 1900s which came to full flower during the Sexual Revolution of the 1960s, fueled by the Pill, penicillin, and abortion on demand. Recall that the economic law of supply and demand states that the lower the price for an item, the higher the demand. By lowering the cost of sex outside of marriage, demand increased, putting America on the path to becoming a low sexual restraint (LSR) culture. By way of illustration, in 1900 there were thirteen marriages to every divorce; a mere hundred years later, there were just two![116] Please stop and consider the immensity of that change, for it is simply astounding and has widespread cultural ramifications.

As a culture casts off sexual restraint and transitions to a low sexual restraint (LSR) culture, the formerly innocuous hypergamy turns malevolent. Homely Harriett, who happily married Sam in the HSR culture, discovers that she can entice the Quarterback into her orb with her sexual wiles. Yes, sex is a powerful magnet indeed, and the Quarterback is a more-than-willing participant, but the Quarterback sees Harriett as nothing more than life support for her vagina, the most convenient semen receptacle of the moment; while, at the same time, Harriett's hypergamous nature often allows her to rationalize away his intentions, misconstruing his mere sexual appetite for genuine attraction.

> *By way of illustration, in 1900 there were thirteen marriages to every divorce; a mere hundred years later, there were just two!*

When the Quarterback predictably dumps Harriett, one might hope that she would learn from her mistakes, but that is not often the case, for the thrill of the Quarterback's attentions is strong, virginity given is gone, and Harriett looks for her next thrill with a man above her marital reach, and then the next.

Homely Harriett graduates high school with a partner count of five to a dozen men and might well double down over the next few years as she enjoys her youth, her willing vagina overcoming her homely looks regularly as the party winds down. But every new

---

[116] United States Department of Health and Human Services, National Center for Health Statistics.

sexual partner further conditions Harriett, her hypergamy having transformed her from a woman who could have been a good mother and a perfectly fine wife for Steady Sam into a woman who Sam wouldn't (at least shouldn't) even consider marrying, thereby leaving her with the poorest of prospects as her youth wanes. If Harriett marries, she likely divorces and, if she escapes the endless joys of single motherhood, she will have to be content with Oprah, cats, genital herpes, and poverty into her old age. She will die lonely, embittered, impoverished, and guilt-laden over her likely aborted son.

As sad as Harriett's culturally-encouraged but self-made situation might be, her choices don't affect her alone. To the contrary, the Quarterback uses Harriett's availability to apply not-so-subtle pressure on other women to perform sexually or find themselves summarily dumped. Many will succumb to the pressure, societal sexual restraint receding apace, one unmarried virgin at a time. All is not lost, for Satan is pleased and the Quarterback finds himself very sexually satisfied through a great variety of young women, as do the remaining highly desirable men, the alphas, but Sam and most of his ilk are alone, frustrated, sexless, and often addicted to porn as their sole sexual release, reading with anticipation Internet articles about soon-to-be-released sex robots advertised to be as sexually fulfilling as the real thing but without the baggage or the diseases. Plus, Sam can purchase a virgin robot. The West (along with China and India) will soon enough discover that a large, sex-starved, male populace is harmful to its stability and future well-being.

Sam, if he unwisely marries Harriett, is destined for divorce slavery as Harriett's hypergamy draws her to divorce him after the customary five to ten years and two children. If Sam doesn't marry, a man who would've made a good dad is without offspring and without moral sexual relationships. Meanwhile, the Quarterback continues to enjoy easy sexual access to countless women over the following decades, defiling them for marriage merely to satisfy his short-term sexual appetites. Ponder the extent of the damage wrought: An alpha male not restricted by moral considerations and living in a LSR culture might have fifty to a hundred or more sexual partners over his lifetime, while the elite male may enjoy thousands. This scenario, multiplied by millions, sets a society on a near certain path to destruction.

To better illustrate, let's substitute real people in place of our hypothetical ones. In a recent article, Karen Cross wrote the sad tale of her hypergamy, unfortunately a very ordinary and typical story, one that destroyed her marriage and her future.[117] She married young, early in her SMV peak, to Matthew, a man close to her own age. She wrote, "We were desperately in love and had our future life together mapped out." She was a white collar career woman in a "junior role at a women's magazine" while her blue-collar husband "worked fitting tyres and exhausts." She continues, "But as time went on, and my magazine career – and salary – advanced, I started to resent Matthew as he drifted from one dead-end job to another. I still loved him, but I began to feel embarrassed by his blue-collar jobs, annoyed that, despite his intelligence, he didn't have a career." This is textbook hypergamy in action, thinking she'd married below her potential, believing that she could have done better than a man making his living with his hands. "I began to wish he was more sophisticated and earned more. I felt envious of friends with better-off partners," she continues. And in the natural and predictable conclusion, "I stopped seeing Matthew as my equal." Translation: She had lost complete respect for her husband, seeing him as "someone who was holding me back." Why was Karen superior in her own mind to her husband: *career and credentials.*

---

[117] Karen Cross, "I Left the Love of my Life Because I Thought I Could Do Better. Now I'm Childless and Alone at 42," *The Daily Mail*, January 16, 2013.

As you should expect, as her respect for Matthew waned, the couple's "sex life had dwindled" as well. Eight years into their relationship, high noon to the hypergamous woman, "I told Matthew I was leaving. We spent hours talking and crying as he tried to convince me to stay, but I was adamant." Her reason for leaving was simply this: She was "convinced there would be another, better Mr. Right waiting around the corner." She was willing to destroy her marriage and deeply wound the man for whom she had publicly promised her love for life in pursuit of a mere upgrade, a more "exciting" man, one worthy of her love. You just can't make this stuff up, but it gets even more revealing: Matthew eventually found a new girlfriend and would no longer talk to his ex-wife. Prepare yourself, dear reader: "I hated the fact Matthew was suddenly putting another woman before me." Yes, that's right, she flushed her husband down the proverbial toilet and then became angry when she was no longer at the top of his priority list.

Karen eventually met her ideal man, a "successful singer" and thought, "I had finally found the excitement and love that I craved." Do you think she was concerned about Matthew while she was sexing it up with her singer? Of course not, but the singer predictably and regularly cheated on her, eventually impregnating another woman and leaving Karen high and dry. Her life then "fell apart" and, surprise, surprise, surprise, she suddenly "realized that Matthew was the only person who had loved and understood me." Translation: "Help! I'm really not going to do better than that embarrassing blue-collar man after all. Agony of agonies. Oh, how I wish I had him back!" She laments, "My decision to leave him has definitely cost me the chance of ever becoming a mother." Karen Cross' wedding vows (and half her sisters') must have been: "To have and to hold from this day forward, for better or worse, for richer or poorer, in sickness and in health, to love and cherish, till death do us part, *unless and until I might do better*." Unfortunately, her sisters are legion.

Hypergamy 68

The results of such decisions are entirely predictable. Quality men aren't pining for past-MED, divorced women, usually raising another man's (or men's) children. Enjoy your cats, Karen.

The man who understands female hypergamy will curb its effects by marrying while approaching or during his SMV peak, will marry "within his means," and will work to keep his SMV high in his wife's eyes.

PARTNER COUNT MATTERS

One of the most striking differences between a cat and a lie is that a cat has only nine lives.[118]
— Pudd'nhead Wilson's Calendar

Just as women are the gatekeepers to sex, men are the gatekeepers to commitment. The less a woman has guarded her gate, the more a man needs to guard his. The Christian man (and any other man wishing to avoid divorce slavery) will open his gate of commitment slowly and with great caution, treating it more like a bank vault – alarm off, clock at 7:30 and timer lock disengaged, 4 turns counterclockwise to 91, three turns clockwise to 44, two turns counterclockwise to 19, back to 79, bank manager's key turned, security guard's key turned, retract the cylinders, and then think about whether to open the vault door or just lock it back.

One marker to seriously reflect upon before even removing the reinforcement bar from the commitment gate is your prospective

---

[118] Mark Twain, *Pudd'nhead Wilson* (Dover Publications, 1999, originally published in 1894), page 30.

wife's previous sexual partner count, or N, for short. The higher her N, the less suitable she is for making and keeping the marriage commitment. From a study with a sample size of ten thousand women, it was revealed that eighty per cent of women who married as virgins (or with no other sexual partners besides their husbands) were still in stable marital relationships after five years.[119] For women with just one sexual partner other than their husband, that number dropped to just above fifty percent. For women with five or more non-marital partners, the stable marriage number dropped below thirty percent! Think, men. Your risk of becoming a divorce slave increases *dramatically* if your wife has had sexual relations with just one other man. Just one! And the chance of enjoying a stable marriage continues to decrease inexorably as her N increases. Bottom line: Marry a chaste woman and you have an eighty percent chance of a successful marriage; marry a slut and you have an eighty percent chance of a failed marriage! For the few mathematically challenged who might be reading this book, marry a chaste woman and there is a four out of five chance that you'll remain married after five years. Marry a slut, and there is a four out of five chance that you'll be divorced. Do you want to roll the dice with your future (and your children's future) against those poor odds? Do you wish to invite divorce slavery? By no means! Just look at the chart of this same data.

> *Think, men. Your risk of becoming a divorce slave increases dramatically if your wife has had sexual relations with just one other man. Just one!*

---

[119] Robert E. Rector et al., *The Harmful Effects of Early Sexual Activity and Multiple Sexual Partners Among Women: A Book of Charts* (Washington DC: The Heritage Foundation, June 23, 2003).

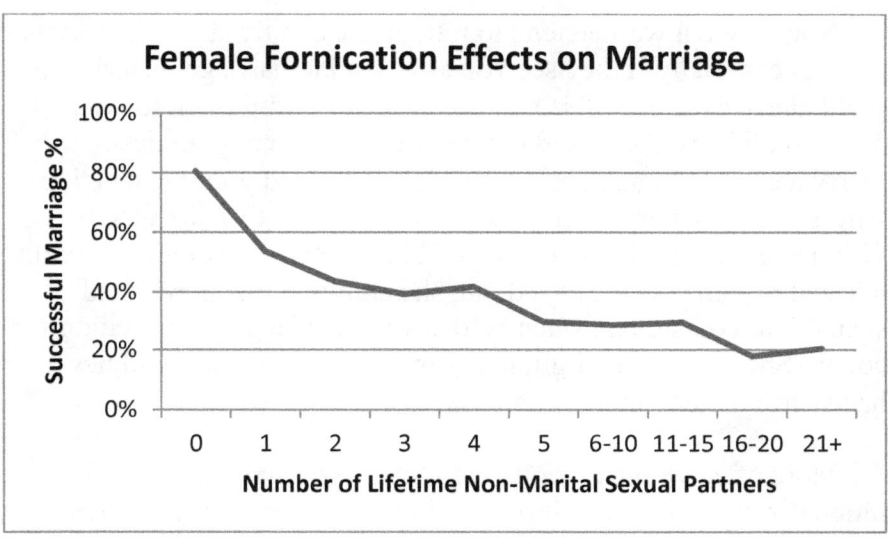

I hope it's been sufficiently demonstrated that if you are considering a woman as possible marriage material, you *must* understand her sexual history. In the best case, it's a non-story or a very short story, and she's a virgin. In case you were not aware, God provided a wonderful physical marker for a woman's purity: the hymen. If her hymen is intact, it is virtually assured that she is a virgin, a new surgical procedure, namely hymenoplasty, notwithstanding. (That's right, doctors are now conspiring with women to defraud their new husbands, allowing a busy woman to possess a reconstructed hymen to better perpetrate her fraud, providing iron-clad false evidence of her supposed virginity. One surgeon's website invites women to: "Find out how you can reclaim your virginity through hymenoplasty.") If she's a virgin, your first sexual encounter will cause her pain and bleeding, and she will likely be a bit embarrassed about the entire act. If she's not a verifiable virgin, your next step is to understand and verify her sexual history.

Non-virginal women tend to rationalize and lie about their sexual history, especially if they see you as potential marriage material, and particularly once they discover that chastity is important to you. You would be well-advised to withhold expressing your desire to marry a chaste woman until after you understand your prospective wife's sexual history. I once had a woman insist that she was a virgin even though I knew that she'd been having sex regularly with a friend of mine. Once called out, she admitted that they'd had sexual intercourse, but, since he'd always used a condom, it didn't count. She was still a virgin in her own mind because she'd never had sperm in her vagina.

More often women won't be quite so open and silly in their rationalizations, but definitions are important, and many women won't count sexual liaisons that end short of full intercourse or even full intercourse when such dalliances might be considered of an excusable nature. For example, she might not count sex as sex if she was drunk, or if it was a "mistake," or if it was only a one night stand, or what have you. You see, twelve minus nine is only three and three doesn't sound so bad in today's LSR world. The woman who's had a dozen partners in full sexual intercourse magically has had only three as far as her potential future husband knows: prom night with her high school boyfriend (I didn't intend to get drunk, really), once at the beginning of her college freshman year when she was taken advantage of at a fraternity rush party by two men (this counts as only one partner since she will fail to mention the second man she had on the same night), and her long-time boyfriend in her junior year of college (and they were engaged!) There, that's not too bad, is it? Know that if she's willing to lie, it will be a very well put together lie.

In a recent "Dear Bel" column,[120] the British equivalent of Ann Landers, a woman wrote:

Dear Bel,

When I met my husband 40 years ago I knew he was 'the one.' He had firm opinions on sex before marriage (outdated even then) and was a virgin.

As I got to know him, it became clear that he'd never consider marrying somebody with 'history.' He thought sex special and wouldn't want to imagine his wife having it with others.

But, by 22, I'd been having sex for four years. Madly in love and wanting him to marry me, I lied.

He was bound to realise I wasn't a virgin, so I made up a story that I'd been in a long engagement, giving up my virginity under pressure only a month before my wedding day, then reluctantly had sex twice with my fiancé, who then dumped me, leaving me devastated and ashamed.

He was very understanding and proposed soon after. We married and moved to his home town — a relief, as I'd worried we might bump into a friend who might speak out of turn.

This woman enticed a man into marriage by lying (and maintaining that lie) for forty years, concealing a busy past that she knew would disqualify her from his consideration for marriage. *This is fraud.* But one day an old friend stopped by to visit and, thinking her husband was outside, "Inevitably, we talked of the past," probably laughing about the good times had by all concerned.

---

[120] "Dear Bel," *The Daily Mail*, November 2, 2012.

Unbeknownst to her, her husband was actually in the home reading and overheard the entire conversation. He's filing for divorce. She defends herself, "He's a man of principle, and I have hurt him, but not in a bad cause. I just wanted to spend my life with him all those years ago. I won't be the only woman who ever lied about her sexual history."

Those men of principle are a dastardly lot, expecting veracity within the marriage covenant is too much to expect. Indeed. Though she lived a lie, her last sentence rings true. You would be absolutely stunned with the scale and sophistication of the lies I've seen put forth by women to secure commitment from a man: as a path to a green card, access to financial resources, or to secure long-term financial resources through false paternity. "I find more bitter than death the woman who is a snare, whose heart is a trap and whose hands are chains."[121] Forewarned is forearmed.

Also, be extremely skeptical of the rape story. As vile as actual rape might be, in the hands of a non-virginal woman wishing to present herself as chaste to entice a man to commitment, it represents the magical fairy dust that explains the absence of her hymen and simultaneously absolves her of any responsibility in the matter. Rape stories are very, very common when women are actively concealing a busy past. I personally know of a good man whose wife put him into divorce slavery after a twenty year marriage for the usual rationalizations (he was a very controlling man, don't you see), and shortly afterward she began dating the man who'd supposedly stolen her virginity via "rape" during her college years. Odd that she'd seek out and date her rapist of twenty years before, isn't it? I only hope her former "rapist" is not too "controlling." Of course, only she knows how many other "rapists" knew her before she met her Steady Sam. It's too bad this book wasn't available at

---

[121] Ecclesiastes 7:26

that time; Sam and his future children could have been spared tragedy.

If a woman of some interest claims rape in her past, ask her who raped her. Ask her if she told her father about the rape. Ask her if she reported the rape to authorities. If not, why not? If she can't answer these questions to your full satisfaction, there likely wasn't a rape, only a rape story. Post-coital regret doesn't transform consensual sexual intercourse into rape. Let her lies and proclivities ruin some other man's life. If you're interested in a woman who was genuinely raped, especially if sexually abused as a child, the crimes committed against her, though genuine and tragic, will still impact your marriage, so, before marriage, take due care to ensure that she's worked through those past traumas to the extent that it's possible to do so.

You don't have to be a private investigator to confirm her sexual history as indicators abound: If her friends are high N, she is likely high N. If they party hard, she is likely high N. If she belongs to a sorority or is a "little sis" to a fraternity, she's more likely to be high N. If she gets drunk, she's likely high N. If you hear a story of her sneaking out of her parent's home at night, she's likely high N. If she won't take you back to her hometown or seeks to control to whom you speak while there, she's more likely high N. I could go on. Use your common sense. As Ronald Reagan was famous for saying, "Trust but verify."

The corollary function is the higher her N, the higher the chance she'll commit adultery, and the higher the chance she will become pregnant by another man during your marriage, leaving you cuckolded and unknowingly pouring your time, talent, and treasure into raising another man's child. Known paternity in a social environment increases the commitment level of fathers. Conversely, the lower the confidence of paternity, the lower the commitment level of fathers. Tragically, the extremely LSR culture prevalent in the inner cities of the United States provides a living, breathing laboratory for this theory and these same destructive pathologies are now rapidly expanding within other communities as well. Though you may have limited influence on the greater population, you can at least take all measures to ensure that your own marriage is stable, producing healthy children of known paternity in spite of the nation's LSR culture, propagating the remnant.

The simple summary is this: The higher a woman's N count, the likelier you are to end up in divorce slavery, as past behavior is an imperfect but good predictor of future behavior. The women who've bought into the feminist myth will have spent their twenties on career and playing the field (translation: having casual sex with many alpha men.) You now understand these dangers. Dismiss such a woman with prejudice; do not commit; divorce slavery ahead! This issue is significantly exacerbated when a low N man marries a high N woman. Though marrying a high N woman is risky for any man, a low N man should never even consider doing so.

Now that you better understand the effects of partner count on a woman's future family and marriage, let me encourage you to keep this in mind when temptation rears its destructive head. The successful man living in an LSR culture will face sexual temptations regularly, but the Christian man should give such temptation no quarter. Instead, he should seek to cultivate not merely long time preferences but, modeling after our Lord, eternal ones. For God's sake, for your sake, for her sake, for society's sake, do not defile another man's future bride and thereby weaken his future marriage. As physically satisfying as it might be in the moment, she's simply not yours to have. I repeat, *she's simply not yours to have*. Fornication is a sin with eternal consequences. The man committed to sexual purity must keep in mind that sexual arousal diminishes self-control. It's not difficult to understand that if you allow yourself to sexually advance with a willing woman, you'll likely fail to control your sex drive. Don't do it! God through Solomon provides specific warning regarding the adulterous: "Keep to a path far from her, do not go near the door of her house, lest you give your best strength to others and your years to one who is cruel, lest strangers feast on your wealth and your toil enrich another man's house."[122] These are the very consequences of marrying poorly, observably and reliably ending in divorce slavery.

It's worth repeating that the Apostle Paul brings special emphasis to sexual sin: "Flee from sexual immorality. All other sins a man commits are outside his body, but he who sins sexually sins against his own body."[123] It's not an unforgivable sin since Jesus Himself explicitly forgave a woman caught in the very act of adultery: "Neither do I condemn thee: go, and sin no more."[124] Jesus ministered to women who'd fallen to sexual temptation. Indeed, God will forgive those who seek forgiveness and

> ***Fornication is a sin with eternal consequences.***

repent from their sins, for "as far as the east is from the west, so far has he removed our transgressions from us."[125] He even forgets our transgressions: "I, even I, am he who blots out your transgressions, for my own sake, and remembers your sins no more."[126] If you've sinned, seek God's forgiveness, and *sin no more.* His forgiveness doesn't necessarily remove the wake we've created through our sins, their natural consequences, but He will help us navigate through our own mess, even redeem our mistakes in others' lives if we'll repent. If you've had a baby out of wedlock, you still have the baby, but, if

---

[122] Proverb 5:8
[123] 1 Corinthians 6:18
[124] John 8:11b, Darby translation
[125] Psalm 103:12
[126] Isaiah 43:25

you repent, God will not hold your sins against you and will welcome you into eternity. That's the reason He came, to save sinners like me and you and the Apostle Paul: "Here is a trustworthy saying that deserves full acceptance: Christ Jesus came into the world to save sinners – of whom I am the worst."[127] Thanks be to God! If He can save the "worst," He can save you.

---

[127] 1 Timothy 1:15

CAREER AND CREDENTIALS

Negative feedback is the process of coupling the output back in such a way as to cancel some of the input.[128]
— Paul Horowitz

Most women today are trained to value career over family and the more your wife values her career, the higher the chances she'll divorce you. According to a British study, "Working women are more than three times more likely to be divorced than their stay-at-home counterparts," and "the longer hours women work, the more likely they are to be divorced."[129] Of particular interest, a separate study estimates "that having the wife earn more than husband increases the likelihood of divorce by 50 percent."[130]

---

[128] Paul Horowitz and Winfield Hill, *The Art of Electronics* (Cambridge, UK: Cambridge University Press, 1994), page 175.
[129] Roger Dobson, "Working women are more likely to seek divorce," *The Independent*, July 10, 2005.
[130] Marianne Bertrand et al., "Gender identity and relative income within households," February, 2013.

Feminist teachings are core to women chasing their careers since stay-at-home wives and mothers are deemed foolish and unproductive, the feminist equivalent of an Uncle Tom, selling out her sisters. The feminist focus on career has encouraged women to delay marriage, which naturally delays family formation. The later she marries, the fewer children she'll conceive. The smaller a man's family, the higher the chance he'll have no sons, thus reinforcing the negative feedback loop generation-over-generation since fathers without sons tend to press their competitive nature onto their daughters, her increased competitiveness amplifying her focus on credentials and career in the next generation, further exacerbating already falling birth rates. This self-reinforcing negative feedback loop has resulted in a fertility rate *barely one-half* what it was in the late fifties.

Some years ago a female vice-president of a regional bank, in her mid-fifties, requested a sales meeting to discuss my company's banking business. As we became acquainted, the conversation took a turn that I'm sure she wasn't expecting when, prompted by an off-hand comment she'd made, I asked her why she'd been so consumed with business during her life. She admitted that her father pushed her hard to excel, to compete with the boys, to win, and she spent her most fertile and attractive years hustling for the bank. Surprising even herself, she told me that she was living a life of emptiness and regret. How different her life might have been if her dad would have shared the motherhood imperative with his young daughter instead of sending her out to compete with the boys. Knowing no better, he became "That Dad," much to his daughter's future chagrin. Such stories are legion. Don't be That Dad; don't let your daughter live a life of regret out of youthful ignorance and certainly not at your bidding.

Having likewise focused on career during her peak SMV and now age forty-six, Claudia Connell explained her story, "I grew up in Sussex then moved to London to pursue my job as a journalist, where I threw myself into a heady social life."[131] During her fertile years, she'd "shudder at the thought of a living room clogged up with toys," but now joins her barren sisters in lament, their wombs empty by choice: "In my 30s, I really didn't want [children]. It's only now, as the choice is removed, that I begin to wonder what my life would be like with a family." She's is coming to terms with the results of her decision, but too late, "I accept that my opportunity to have a family has gone," and has rightly observed, "A woman over 45 on an internet dating site is made to feel as welcome as a parking ticket. The sites may be full of single men in their 40s, but they sure aren't looking to meet women of the same age!" Her most potent observation is that not one of her single friends "is truly happy being on her own. Suddenly, all those women we pitied for giving up their freedom for marriage and children are the ones feeling sorry for us."

I know the capable daughter of a very competitive man who has imprinted his competitiveness upon her. She excelled in her studies, resulting in her having recently been accepted into a prestigious medical school. This is quite an accomplishment, but there is a looming problem ahead as her self-identified *most important life goal* is to become a wife and mother. Her occupational training is simply incongruous with her stated life goals, the demands of medical school keeping her all but out of the marriage market past her peak SMV. Furthermore, the servicing of her medical school loans will keep her fully occupied past the end of her high fertility window.

If your daughter is naturally competitive and wants to express her competitive desires through athletics or other outlets, that is to be commended and encouraged. But just as the very best coaches tailor their coaching style to each player, so fathers must seek to

---

[131] Claudia Connell, "The lonely legacy of my Sex and the City lifestyle," *The Daily Mail*, November 4, 2012.

observe and understand each child's gifts, encouraging each child, son or daughter, to develop their natural strengths, helping them become what God created them to be instead of what you wished they might become. Though your hopes and desires will often align with God's and your child's natural abilities, you must be open to the idea that this isn't the case and adapt accordingly.

It is generally no sin for a woman to work outside her home, but know that it's quite difficult for your wife to be the best wife and mother when distracted by professional duties. This is not a difficult equation to solve; the hours she's working outside the home are not available for nurturing her children. Many people do not believe one income sufficient to meet their financial objectives, but a well-chosen helpmate will be capable of supporting you sufficiently well that your advancement will more than make up for any monetary income lost by her staying at home. In my own business, I found those men with highly supportive stay-at-home wives were significantly more productive and, on average, commanded a significantly higher income over time. They also appeared to live lives of lower stress and greater happiness.

Just because a woman is working when you meet doesn't necessarily mean she's a career woman. As I was getting acquainted with my bride, she was successful in her chosen career field but made it clear that her highest and best goals were becoming and being a wife and mother. Though talented in her work, she was in her profession to support herself only until she married (or in case she never married.) She hasn't spent one hour earning an income since the day we exchanged our vows and, even at this very moment, she is teaching our younger children in our home school, her efforts being counted to the good for all eternity. Dear God in Heaven, how I love that woman!

One additional nugget for thought: Your wife is commanded to respect you just as you are commanded to love her. A career woman is professionally accountable to respect her boss as part of her duties, a person almost assuredly of higher income and stature. If her boss is male, these circumstances possibly set her up for temptation since respect naturally drives attraction in women. Perhaps in small ways or perhaps in large, her submissive work role may well have a deleterious effect on her ability to maintain her respect for you over time – the lower your relative SMV, the higher the risk of infidelity.

A woman's career goals (or absence of such) are simply one more variable to add to your marriage calculus, one with more ramifications than you might initially surmise. To survive and prosper, society does not *need* women in business, the military, science, or any other place outside of having and raising children. I submit to you the entire history of the United States before 1920 as evidence. Dedicated wives and mothers have a far greater impact on society than women spending their time playing office or writing prescriptions for acne control merely to service their medical school debts. This does not make such activities sinful, just deleterious to the health of marriage, family, and society at large. For a society to thrive and *remain stable over time*, the one thing that women absolutely must do is birth and raise children. Once women's primary goals *en masse* exclude mothering, the society is simply doomed, particularly when its most capable women are having the fewest children. The womb is simply irreplaceable, and demographics are destiny. This is not hard math, merely inconvenient.

> ***Once women's primary goals en masse exclude mothering, the society is simply doomed…***

Let's now briefly consider the importance of credentials in regards to female hypergamy. Remember Karen Cross, the hypergamous woman who dumped her blue-collar husband to spend her last years of high SMV servicing unfaithful musicians, now alone and probably shopping for her third cat? The hypergamous Karens of the world want to be married to the best man possible and, in the feminist orthodoxy, credentials are critical. Female hypergamy all but demands that a woman marry a man who possesses credentials at least equal to her own and the Karens have a bleak future before them. According to an interesting and well-done study,[132] undergraduate men outnumbered women at a ratio of 2.3 to 1 in 1947, that peak primarily driven by the GI bill, but that ratio has been steadily shifting since that time, reaching parity in 1980, and, by 2005, it stood at 1.30 women for each man. Given these long-term trends, many future Karens holding their various credentials and their attendant debts will find themselves married to men who work "fitting tires and exhausts" or other "demeaning" work that merely keeps the country functioning. This does not bode well for the future divorce rates at large. If you find yourself attracted to a woman holding credentials "superior" to yours, take due care.

Beyond hypergamous considerations, obtaining credentials is very expensive, both in time and money, with many incurring substantial debts to obtain them. This debt often becomes a veritable millstone around her neck (and her future husband's), especially for those who incurred large debt to obtain credentials that don't translate into high post-degree incomes. The debt incurred often forces women to focus on their careers, even if they later decide they'd prefer to direct their full-time efforts towards their family. Know that if you marry a woman carrying large debt of any kind, it will take significant time and effort to service and clear that debt at the same time you'll be needing money to establish your home and perhaps your business. Student loan debt is particularly

---

[132] Claudia Goldin et al, "The Homecoming of American College Women: The Reversal of the College Gender Gap," *Journal of Economic Perspectives*, Volume 20, Number 4, Fall 2006, Pages 133 – 156.

malevolent because, just like tax debt, it is not dischargeable in bankruptcy; therefore, if she has student loan debt, it must be retired. Don't forget that such debts must be retired with after-tax dollars, a precious commodity in a high-tax era. Funding an education with debt is volunteering for a modern form of indentured servitude. If you marry her, you marry her debt. If she possesses a degree named with the suffix of "studies," understand that her ability to contribute to the family's income to retire her student loan debt will be limited, particularly in a time when the supply of degrees outstrips the demand. The ever helpful law of supply and demand enlightens us yet again: Just talk to a newly minted law school graduate from anywhere other than a top-tier law school. It's hard to service a six-figure law school debt by processing mortgages or waiting tables.

You should now possess a better understanding of the primary risk factors to consider before unlocking your commitment gate: the age dynamics of sexual market value; the effects of female hypergamy in an LSR culture; the effects of her sexual partner count on stable marriage; the effects of disparate credentials, vis-à-vis female hypergamy; debt effects; and the likely effects of her career aspirations on your marriage and family. The more risk factors she possesses (and the more severe), the higher your risk, and the more scrutiny is warranted. A heavily indebted, high N count career woman with two abortions, three years past her MED, holding a Ph.D. in women's studies, and coming from a broken home, would make for a horrible risk, no matter how much attraction you might have for her rapidly declining SMV, but unwise or ignorant men still marry such women.

This cannot be overstated, so I shall state it again: Past behavior is an imperfect but good predictor of future behavior, and, remember, you *won't be having sex with your ex-wife!* As Dr. James Dobson has stated many times, "The key to a healthy marriage is to keep your eyes wide open before you wed, and then half-closed thereafter."[133] Most do precisely the opposite! True Christian marriage is a lifetime commitment that changes eternity and, even in the feminist world, you are the gatekeeper of commitment. By all means, for yourself, your future wife, and your future children, *be a worthy gatekeeper.*

I shall close this chapter with an important aside: Once you locate a virtuous woman and make her your bride, thank her loving mother and her good father for raising such a woman. You are more indebted to them than anyone on earth beyond your own parents.

---

[133] Ben Franklin is credited with a similar statement.

SHE REALLY DOES THINK DIFFERENTLY THAN YOU DO

Together, these findings support the view of a sexual dimorphism that manifested in the recruitment of gender-specific neural resources during the successful deployment of self-control.[134]
— *Esther K. Diekhof*

Men and women think in profoundly different ways.

A few years ago my family and I visited the Garden of the Gods in Colorado Springs on the first day of rock climbing after a temporary prohibition due to nesting raptors. It was a beautiful day, and climbers were everywhere, enjoying the magnificent heights. One particular group was assisting a newbie, an attractive young woman who was clearly distressed by the thought of technical

---

[134] Esther K. Diekhof et al., "A functional neuroimaging study assessing gender differences in the neural mechanisms underlying the ability to resist impulsive desires," *Brain Research*, September 14, 2012.

climbing, but peer pressure prevailed, and up she went with assistance and encouragement. Not too far into her climb she became paralyzed by fear and faced a dilemma. I learned a bit about women (at least about that woman) on that day. A man in fear and not willing to proceed would generally have just stated the obvious, "Hey guys, I was nuts for trying this. Heights do not agree with me, and I need to come back down." He would have taken his ribbing but all would have remained friends, and he would have preserved a modicum of respectability. Not this poor woman. She could not, would not, admit her obvious fear, but could not make herself go one foot higher, so she lied, and poorly: "I can't take any more altitude. The air is thinner up here and I just can't breathe. Let me down. Get me down so I can breathe again!" She was less than twenty feet off the ground. An athletic basketball player might have been able to touch her feet. At first I thought surely she must've meant the altitude of Colorado Springs didn't agree with her but, no, once she was back down on terra firma she stated with relief, "I'm better now. The dense air is helping me breathe." I still chuckle when thinking about her.

Though this is an extreme and silly example, your wife (or future wife) really does think differently that you do, and you must understand the difference. The observant man has known throughout all history that men and women process stimuli and react in dissimilar manners, but the mind has always been what software developers call a "black box," meaning we can observe the behavior and draw some conclusions but don't really understand the causes of what we observe. Alas, technology has advanced, and we're now getting at least a peek into the "black box" of the human mind. In a recent study led by Professor Ragini Verma out of the University of Pennsylvania, a team examined nearly a thousand human brains using a technique called diffusion tensor imaging. The result is a "neural map of the brain." The map of the male brain versus the female brain, what the professor calls the "connectome," is striking.

She stated, "In women most of the connections go between left and right across the two hemispheres while in men most of the connections go between the front and back of the brain."[135] Male brains are quite literally wired differently than female brains.

In separate research, Esther K. Diekhof and Oliver Gruber performed a fascinating experiment using functional magnetic resonance imaging (fMRI) technology to better understand how the brain "mediates the balance between proximal reward desiring and long-term goals."[136] In layman's terms, they wanted to better understand what happens in the brain when faced with a conflict between short-term gratification and long-term goals, what they termed a "desire-reason dilemma." Examining gender as a variable was not part of the original study; however, at some point during their work, they began noticing differences between how men's and women's brains appeared to function when faced with a desire-reason dilemma. To more fully explore and verify this observation, they designed a subsequent experiment and found that when faced with a desire-reason dilemma men had "an increased frontostriatal coupling" which "helped men to control immediate reward desiring" while "women showed the reverse frontostriatal connectivity." Additionally, they observed that, "during self-control men showed a stronger decrease in some limbic regions than women."[137]

---

[135] Steve Connor, "The hardwired difference between male and female brains could explain why men are 'better at map reading'," *The Independent*, December 3, 2013.

[136] Esther K. Diekhof and Oliver Gruber, "When Desire Collides with Reason: Functional Interactions between Anteroventral Prefrontal Cortex and Nucleus Accumbens Underlie the Human Ability to Resist Impulsive Desires," *The Journal of Neuroscience*, January 27, 2010.

[137] Esther K. Diekhof et al., "A Functional Neuroimaging Study Assessing Gender Differences in the Neural Mechanisms Underlying the Ability to Resist Impulsive Desires," *Brain Research Journal*, Volume 1473, September 14, 2010, pages 63-77.

Summarizing, when faced with a desire-reason dilemma men tend to actively suppress their emotions in favor of reason and logic while women tend to take the opposite approach. Yes, she really does think differently than you do, so don't get upset when she's being what you deem less logical than your computer. It's just the way she's created so, just as I never suggest men should pretend they don't have a strong sex drive because they were created that way, don't expect her to be a female version of Mr. Spock. Who would want to be married to a female Spock anyway? Lead her with *full consideration* of her emotions but, just as a man's strong sex drive doesn't excuse his inability to control himself, a woman's natural tendency to rely on her emotions doesn't excuse her either.

By all means let this knowledge inform how you interact with her, knowing that your mind will gravitate toward reason and hers toward emotion when solving problems. This apparent conflict can work powerfully together as her views inform your own. Just as the very best coaches adapt themselves to their individual players, you will be most effective as a leader when you tailor your leadership style with consideration of those whom you lead. I hope by now you understand that by "tailoring" I don't mean abdicating, not by any means. Still, a man who makes important family decisions without any regard to his wife's thoughts on the matter isn't strengthening his marriage and isn't taking advantage of all his resources. That understood, most substantive decisions are best made using logical analysis, not emotion. As the head of the family, the ultimate responsibility of your family's decisions lands squarely at your feet. The buck stops with you.

God knew what He was doing, for the logical brain is certainly not the best brain for all situations. A single-tasking man immersed in a project might completely forget about his two-year-old son who has wandered off to the neighbor's house, completely unattended. (Not that this has happened to me. I lost one of my daughters instead.) Mark Gungor has his usual humorous take on these differences:

Researchers have discovered that men do, in fact, have the ability to think about absolutely nothing and – get this – still breathe. Neurophysiologist Professor Ruben Gur of the University of Pennsylvania showed that 70 percent of the electrical activity of men's brains shut down when they were in a resting state. Think of that: 70 percent! Women's brains, on the other hand, maintained a full 90 percent of their electrical activity. This demonstrates that women are constantly receiving and analyzing input from their surroundings. Women with children are completely aware of how those children are feeling, what their emotional states are, who their friends are, what their hopes, dreams, and fears are, and if they are plotting any mischief. Contrariwise, men maintain only a vague knowledge deep in the back of their minds that they have a wife and some shorter, nondescript people wandering around.[138]

A good marriage is established by a man and woman, loving each other, committed to each other, and depending upon each other's strengths to balance out their respective weaknesses. When it works well, it's a beautiful relationship that accomplishes much good and greatly pleases God.

---

[138] Mark Gungor, *Laugh Your Way to a Better Marriage* (New York: Atria Paperback, 2008), page 44.

ATTRACTING QUALITY WOMEN

At the end of the day, the best proof of your credibility comes when those who are closest to you and know you the best, love and respect you the most.[139]
— John Maxwell

To be able to choose well, you must first have a choice, making yourself attractive to quality women being the prerequisite that provides choice. Know that living on a mission makes you attractive to women in ways one might not initially surmise. Seek to live a serious mission, strive towards fulfilling it, and you'll naturally have a choice among women. But such complex topics can hardly be adequately summed up in a single paragraph, so let us more fully explore what women genuinely find attractive in a man.

Rule #1: Unless you're happy with loneliness, never bother asking women what they find attractive in a man. You will simply hear what they think they should find attractive, rather than what

---

[139] John C. Maxwell, *Cross-examining Credibility* (The John Maxwell Company, 2011), www.johnmaxwell.com

they actually find attractive, a phenomenon known as social acceptability bias. Instead, it is much more effective to carefully *observe* what actually attracts them. You won't be surprised by some of what you discover: after all, women have been attracted to tall and handsome for ages; however, your observations might surprise you a bit when you discover that, while most women publicly pine for the "Nice Guy," they never end up actually attached to such a man. It's not because Nice Guys are rare, far from it. We are surrounded by them. Many of them even profess their willingness to live in an equalitarian marriage - happy to cook, clean, and do half the dishes – only hoping for an attractive and loyal bride, but they are summarily dismissed and ignored by attractive women as those women chase that which they profess to loathe, the bad boy, Karen Cross' "musician."

Rule #2: The good news for the Christian man is that one needn't be bad to attract women, for women aren't generally attracted to a bad man's nature but, rather, they are attracted to some of his qualities: primarily strength, boldness, and confidence, even irrational confidence. These are good characteristics for every man to possess in measure. The higher your confidence, the wider your influence, the stronger your leadership abilities, the bolder your actions, the more attractive you'll become to women. Though we can speculate as to why women are attracted to these traits, such an understanding is much less important than the simple knowledge that they truly are attracted to these traits.

Kristina Durante[140] performed a very helpful experiment designed to measure women's attraction to bad boys or, using her preferred term, "Sexy Cads." In the experiment the subject women were introduced via video to sets of male "twins" (actually a series

---

[140] Kristina M. Durante et al., "Ovulation Leads Women to Perceive Sexy Cads as Good Dads," *Journal of Personality and Social Psychology*, May 14, 2012.

of single actors posing as twins), each man introducing himself as a potential date. One brother was the classic Nice Guy that Durante termed the Reliable Dad, "socially reserved, not charismatic or adventurous, and explicitly desiring a committed relationship and a family." The Reliable Dad's twin brother, the Sexy Cad, "acted socially dominant, charismatic, and adventurous, while also coming across as unreliable and undependable."

    The women were asked how much parental investment they thought each man might give to his offspring. They were close to evenly split, slightly favoring the Reliable Dad as the man who would invest more in his children unless (and here is where a wise man will pay very close attention) *when the women were nearing ovulation.* That's right. During the peak of her fertility, in the women's eyes the Sexy Cad surged from behind and passed the Reliable Dad by nearly ten percentage points as the one more likely to invest in his future children. Let me emphasize, it's not that they merely found him more attractive, they found him more likely to invest in his children. This is astonishing. What sane person would ever think that the Sexy Cad would invest more in his offspring than the Reliable Dad? The answer: No one, except a woman at the peak of her fertility window. Her hormonal cycles truly do impact her thinking. Of particular note, this surge was muted unless the women were led to believe that they would be the one having his child. They could see through the Sexy Cad (to an extent) when not ovulating or if asked about a child he might have with another woman, but their perceptions were skewed significantly at their fertility peak when considering a man who might father their own child. Durante's experiments demonstrated "how, when, and why ovulation can lead Mr. Wrong to appear like Mr. Right." Don't forget that the "identical twins" looked exactly the same other than their clothing.

Reinforcing Durante's findings, Martie Haselton has noted similar patterns in her team's work at UCLA, finding that, "Women with the really good, stable guy felt more distant at high-fertility periods than low-fertility periods. That isn't the case with women who were mated to particularly sexually attractive men. The closeness of their relationships got a boost just prior to ovulation."[141] Haselton calls "the urge for a stable long-term partner along with increased desire for a more sexually attractive mate during periods of high fertility the 'dual mating hypothesis.'" There are significant implications from these findings. If your bride or a woman you're considering for marriage is less attracted to you during the high-fertility part of her cycle, it's an indication that she might be settling for you, not genuinely attracted to you. I hope by now you understand that such behavior bodes poorly for your marriage or future marriage prospects. Conversely, if she appears most attracted to you during her peak fertility window, it indicates that she generally does find you attractive, and the odds of a successful marriage improve. The observant man can draw conclusions regarding his particular situation after a few months of careful observation.

So who are these Sexy Cads, these alpha men who women find so attractive? They are often (but not always) handsome men, they are near-universally dominant, and they are successful, often leading men in their professional endeavors. Such men naturally and easily attract pretty women, the most obvious being high-profile athletes, popular musicians, and actors. Know that a man doesn't have to be in the top 1% of men to attract quality women, but those who are most successful have many of the same traits, and you can intentionally model some or all of these traits until they become your own.

---

[141] "When she says, 'It's not you, it's me,' it really might be you, UCLA study suggests," *UCLA Newsroom*, October 24, 2012.

Let me be clear: I am not suggesting that you abandon who you are or compromise your beliefs for the purposes of trying to attract women. As a man looking for a quality woman to marry, any pretense you put forth would need to be maintained for decades; however, there is nothing wrong with examining what makes men successful, learning from them, and then genuinely working to make yourself into a more successful man, a more attractive man. After all, an ambitious man will strive for success in a favored endeavor by reading, practicing, learning, and doing. Why should any aspect of life, particularly one as important as marriage, be off-limits to a man's best efforts? It shouldn't. Yet men who'll spend years refining their professional skills and abilities or their hobbies will walk into the minefield of female relationships with but a few ideas from their mommies, most of which will be the opposite of correct. It's ludicrously stupid. You'll have a much better chance to attract and keep a quality woman if you understand what women find attractive and work, to whatever degree you wish, to genuinely make yourself into an attractive man. If you're capable of reading and understanding this book, you're capable of improving your lot, of increasing your SMV and maintaining it at that higher level. If you're currently at an SMV of 5, wouldn't putting in the effort to raise that to a 7 be a worthwhile investment of time and energy to help secure your future happiness? Hmmm, yes, at least for those men with a pulse.

Not surprisingly in an LSR culture, men have been studying these female attraction patterns to develop and fine-tune strategies for the primary purpose of maximizing their number of short-term sexual partners. One need not endorse their lifestyles to acknowledge that some of them are keen observers of the socio-sexual marketplace. These men purposefully exude confidence beyond reason, actively demonstrate dominance, subtly undermine a woman's self-worth (thereby raising his relative worth in her eyes), intentionally surround themselves with other desirable women (often role-playing friends), exhibit substantial resources (whether they possess them or not), often work hard to keep themselves in top physical form, and become experts in how to interact with women in ways that create sexual desire. Female attraction has some constants so, even though the cad's techniques seek immoral ends, many of their observations can be employed by the moral man to attract quality women, but with one major difference: Since the cad seeks only short-term sexual release, he need only maintain these attractants until he beds his next target, while the moral man's attractiveness must be maintained during a lifetime marriage. In other words, the cad need only pretend, while the moral man must actually become the man to whom women are attracted. Still, the cad's techniques are studied and effective. Take, for example, their technique of surrounding themselves with other attractive women. This works without doubt, but why?

> *Of the women who believed he was available, 59% were interested in a relationship, but of the women who were told he was taken, 90% were interested.*

Rule #3: Women value other women's opinions to a great degree in general and this includes opinions regarding men. The more attention a man secures from desirable women, the more attractive he becomes to other desirable women. Need evidence? In a study that examined this phenomenon, groups of women were provided a photograph of the same man, half of whom were told he was single and half that he was already involved with another woman. Of the women who believed he was available, 59% were interested in a relationship, but of the women who were told he was taken, 90% were interested.[142] Interestingly, the researchers stated, "As

---

[142] Andy Coghlan, "It's true: all the taken men are best," *New Scientist*, August 17, 2009.

predicted, single women were more interested in poaching an attached man rather than pursuing a single man."[143] Let us linger here for a moment and understand this phenomenon: Six out of ten women were interested in a particular man when he was supposedly unattached, leaving four who were not interested. This very same man, once he was supposedly in a relationship (in other words, approved by another woman), nine out of ten women were interested in him. Merely by already being in a relationship, therefore marked as approved by another woman, this man increased the percentage of women interested in him by 50%.

Rule #4: Live on a mission; live life to the full. As previously mentioned, given that the moral man is seeking a lifetime marriage, traits that attract women must be genuinely incorporated into his life. Living one's life on a mission naturally builds *genuine* confidence as skills are mastered and goals met. *Competence builds confidence; confidence attracts.*

The men with choices, more attractive choices, are those with confidence and resources, who actively shape their surroundings (acting upon instead of being acted upon) and exude leadership abilities. As Mr. Beaver said of Aslan the great lion, "He's wild you know. Not like a tame lion."[144] You shouldn't be tame either. Rather, be a bit dangerous, as Mr. Beaver also responded: "Safe? Don't you hear what Mrs. Beaver tells you? Who said anything about safe? 'Course he isn't safe. But he is good."[145] Be like Aslan.

---

[143] Jessica Parker and Melissa Burkley, "Who's chasing whom? The impact of gender and relationship status on mate poaching," *Journal of Experimental Social Psychology*, Volume 45, Number 4, July 2009.

[144] C.S. Lewis, *The Lion, the Witch, and the Wardrobe* (New York: The Macmillan Company, 1950), page 168.

[145] Ibid, page 77.

Risk-taking leaders of other men are pure catnip to women and, as demonstrated above, men accompanied by attractive women find it much easier to attract others. Let me stress: it's quite possible for the Christian man to morally employ these astute observations to his and his future progeny's betterment. The corollary lesson is that apathy, listlessness, and laziness don't build competence and are extremely unattractive to worthy women of any stripe. The lazy man is often a lonely man. Be a good man, a bold man, an energetic man, but never a safe and predictable man. "For God did not give us a spirit of timidity, but a spirit of power, of love and of self-discipline."[146]

A man's sexual market value changes over time. I hope it's clear by now that you can impact your SMV, no matter your age, no matter your station. You can lower your SMV by adding twenty pounds or by coming home every night and telling your wife how scary and unfair you find the world, or you can increase it through all manner of attraction-driving, confidence-inspiring acts. Though a high SMV has obvious utility for the single man, the married man who invests in increasing his SMV will be rewarded as well: with a better marriage, a higher probability of a lifetime marriage, and more regular sex. This, dear reader, is not a bad list.

---

[146] 2 Timothy 1:7

HER ACTIONS SPEAK LOUDER THAN HER WORDS

There are only two kinds of people in the end: those who say to God, "Thy will be done," and those to whom God says, in the end, "Thy will be done." All that are in Hell, choose it.[147] — C.S. Lewis

There was once a man named Jack who loved his high school sweetheart, Jill. He was a handsome man, a good man, an extremely intelligent man, and they seemed destined to live happily ever after. They married right after college. He went on to earn his master's degree in a rigorous STEM field, landed a great job with one of the world's largest corporations, his intelligence and hard work quickly rewarded with increased pay and responsibilities. They had the requisite two kids, built a new home in the suburbs, ate steak and drank good wine, and were living the American dream. Several years into their marriage Jill desired to return to work and began working at the local bank. Unbeknownst to Jack, shortly thereafter Jill began an affair with her boss, a man not even in the same quality

---

[147] C.S. Lewis, *The Great Divorce*, (Great Britain: G. Bles, 1946), page 72.

stratosphere as her husband, but obviously one to whom she was attracted, likely by way of his authority over her.

Jack was eventually promoted to an out-of-state position, moving his family and building an even nicer and much larger home. Thanksgiving Day came to their new home, and Jill's parents drove the ten hours to celebrate with their family. By all accounts it was a fine holiday, food galore, well-prepared, a good day of celebration. While many make Thanksgiving into a four day weekend, not Jack. Work beckoned on Friday morning, and he dutifully headed into the office.

My phone rang at 6 o'clock on that very Friday evening, the day after Thanksgiving. I shall never forget it. Jack had arrived home after work to find his house bare and empty but for his clothes and a cryptic note from his wife explaining that she needed "some space" and had moved back home with her parents, taking his children and most all of their belongings. This was a move that had been planned with aforethought and malice, movers at the ready, starting as soon as Jack left his home. Not surprisingly, Jack found out the next morning that Jill had cleaned out the bank account as well.

Jack was absolutely dumbstruck. He didn't know anything was even wrong beyond day-to-day issues and couldn't fathom that his marriage was so troubled it warranted her leaving. He drove the ten hours to see her, to try to understand what had gone wrong, literally begging her to return home and work on identifying and solving their marital problems. In response, she reiterated that she just needed some time and space. He also sought professional counseling, trying to understand what he could do to repair the relationship from afar.

It was all for naught because, as it turns out, it really was about time and space, not the time to reflect and look for healing but, rather, the time to establish residency in her parent's state. On that fateful day, Jack received an invitation from the out-of-state court regarding the dissolution of his marriage. Her pretenses shown to be lies, Jill's actions came into full focus: This entire charade was just about money and control, and her parents' state had better divorce laws to secure cash and prizes than did her marital home. The "time and space" was all Kabuki theatre: Jack was played to the end as only a good man can be, destined to become a divorce slave, while Jill's parents were complicit in the entire sordid scene, shocking and destroying a good man, the father of their grandchildren, and removing his children forever from his daily guidance. I cannot fathom how it is possible to share a Thanksgiving Day meal with a man you know you're about to gut. When Jill later married her illicit lover, all the pieces fell into place, but too late for Jack and too late for his children, forcibly removed from their father whom they loved.

Jack is a real man and, though sufficiently vague to mask his true identity, this is a true story right down to the smallest detail. I could just as easily used other examples since, sadly, many of these details are all but the norm for a deserting wife. When it comes to relationships, women can be as calculatingly cruel as any man has ever been thought to be.

> *When it comes to relationships, women can be as calculatingly cruel as any man has ever been thought to be.*

As I hope you've gathered by now, I am asserting and have provided significant evidence that most everything you've been taught about women since your childhood is wrong. Despite their pretty faces, shiny hair, and fancy curves, they are no less capable of sin than any man, yet society in general – and Nice Guys in particular – tend to put women on pedestals by default. Men do themselves (and their wives) a great disservice when they place their wives upon a pedestal. When you hear the words "my better half" emanate from a man's mouth, he has very likely placed his wife on just such a pedestal, to both his and her detriment. People tend to believe the propaganda over time but we must not forget: "And Adam was not the one deceived; it was the woman who was deceived and became a sinner."[148] Not that Adam wasn't culpable: "When the woman saw that the fruit of the tree was good for food and pleasing to the eye, and also desirable for gaining wisdom, she took some and ate it. She also gave some to her husband, *who was with her*, and he ate it."[149] Adam was there! Rather than protecting Eve from the Evil One's influence, Adam let her listen to the tempter's lies and half-truths, then *followed* her into sin. His was a failure of leadership, for one cannot lead while following. Most men follow in Adam's footsteps.

When it comes down to interacting with women, attracting quality women, and creating a strong marriage, detached observation is among the most important tools in your toolbox. When a woman complains that she just can't find a man who cares for her while she's having wild sex with a tatted-up biker or her married boss (or both), one should be inclined to apply a higher weight to her actions than her words. When women willingly and *en masse* throw perfectly good and loyal husbands into the divorce court's maw, one must weigh their collective actions and let it inform one's individual choices.

Let us examine but one example of the dichotomy between what men are taught about women and their observable actions. Women often complain that men just do not hold up their end of the bargain when it comes to household duties. When a Nice Guy is confronted with such an accusation he is likely to weigh it and find it true. And

---

[148] 1 Timothy 2:14
[149] Genesis 3:6

it generally is true, but what would the average Nice Guy do about it, and how would he be rewarded or penalized for his actions?

Since the Nice Guy wants a happy wife and a good marriage, he'll often oblige her requests: washing dishes, cooking meals, changing diapers, and whatever else needs done. These changes are often genuinely appreciated by his wife but unconsciously she realizes and notes that his changes came from her direction, implying control and subtly diminishing her respect for him. As we've already covered, a woman's respect for her husband is inversely correlated to her ability to control him.

This doesn't mean that you can never lift a finger to help your loving bride (not at all!), but the wise husband will be a keen observer of his wife's circumstances on a regular and routine basis. He must lead! If he finds her genuinely in need of assistance, as many young mothers truly are, then he should help her (or secure help for her) in whatever ways that are within his means but, BUT, the good and godly husband will take care to meet her needs while not diminishing her respect for him, since maintaining this respect is vitally important to maintaining a healthy, lifetime marriage, to everyone's benefit. Think long term. Have long-term time preferences. Love her well, but wisely. Be proactive, not reactive. Lead.

A recent study published by Sabino Kornrich found that there is an inverse correlation between the amount of "core" housework (meaning housework traditionally performed by women) performed by the husband and the observed frequency of sexual activity in that marriage.[150] Translation: The more domesticated you become, the less respect you'll garner and the less sex you will enjoy. Without scientific corroboration of any sort whatever, I make the naked

---

[150] Sabino Kornrich et al., "Egalitarianism, Housework, and Sexual Frequency in Marriage," *American Sociological Review*, 2012 78(1) pages 26-50.

assertion that having regular and frequent sexual relations with his wife is vitally important to any man who's not dead. Do I hear an amen? Actually, this assertion does have biblical support as Paul exhorts those with less self-control than he (this includes you and me): "Do not deprive each other [of sexual relations] except by mutual consent and for a time, so that you may devote yourselves to prayer."[151] Translation: Enjoy sexual relations frequently with your wife except for specific, understood, and agreed to circumstances: namely, prayer.

When you examine the chart below you'll note that the sex-housework correlation was significant. Kornrich describes this relationship in the way that only a man with a Ph.D. would: "These effects are statistically significant and substantively large. Overall, these results suggest that sexuality is governed by enactments of femininity and masculinity through appropriately gendered performances of household labor that coincide with sexual scripts organizing heterosexual desire."[152]

---

[151] 1 Corinthians 7:5
[152] Sabino Kornrich et al., "Egalitarianism, Housework, and Sexual Frequency in Marriage," *American Sociological Review*, 2012 78(1) pages 26-50.

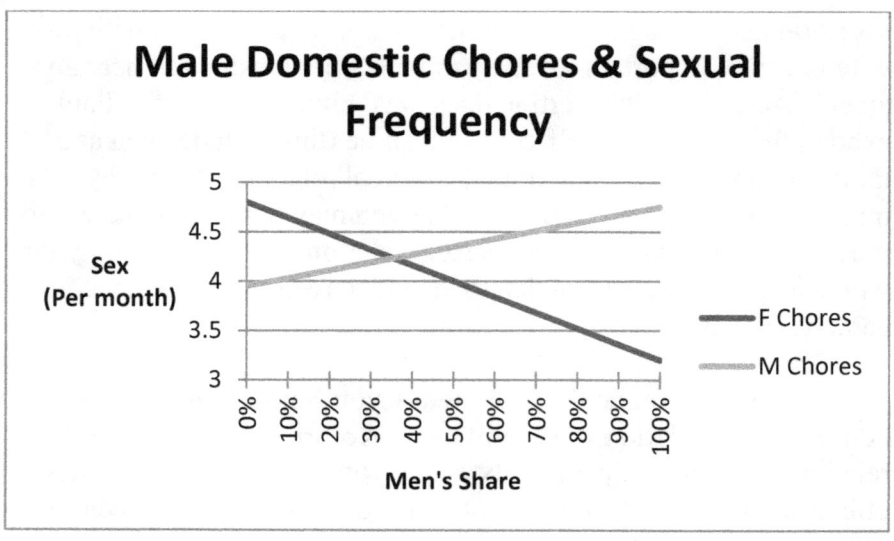

Though minor in importance, the following details from the study are noted purely for entertainment purposes: There was a negative correlation between sexual frequency and educational attainment (poor Kornrich and his Ph.D.) Happily for me and my ilk, there was a positive correlation between sexual frequency and those self-identifying as "Conservative Christian," so now you have yet another way to entice an unredeemed man to join you for church. An even higher positive correlation was for those who self-identified as "Black Protestant." Unless you're black, there's not much to do but envy your black brethren, but if you're a black Catholic, by all means, convert. Yet the world thinks Christians undersexed prudes! Poor atheists.

In addition to considering the negative correlation of men performing core domestic chores and sexual frequency, please note the important *positive* correlation between men's performance of traditionally male domestic chores and sexual frequency, you know, the *red line*.[153] So grab those tools men and fix the car or that leaky faucet. If everything is in tip-top shape, click off the bathroom circuit breaker and then "fix it." Yes, I do accept cash, credit cards, and Paypal. Make your remittance proportional to the benefit received. (Note to churchians: From pre-publication focus group testing, it was deemed necessary to state that the bathroom breaker bit is intended merely as a joke, seeking to provide temporary relief from the important, but dry, supporting statistics.)

If this next study doesn't bring a Cheshire grin to your face, you have no sense of humor whatsoever because, as it turns out, there are other benefits of housework: It helps your wife to maintain her girly figure and improve her health by keeping off the excess pounds. According to this hot-off-the-press study:

From 1965 to 2010, there was a large and significant decrease in the time allocated to household management. By 2010, women allocated 25% more time to screen-based media use than household management (i.e., cooking, cleaning, and laundry combined). The reallocation of time from active pursuits (i.e., housework) to sedentary pastimes (e.g., watching TV) has important health consequences. These results suggest that the decrement in HMEE [household management and energy expenditure] may have contributed to the increasing prevalence of obesity in women during the last five decades.[154]

Isn't it fascinating that so many people waste the time gained via modern conveniences on modern contrivances? Freed to accomplish so much, we often choose to accomplish nothing, or worse.

---

[153] I fully understand the difference between causation and correlation. The observations noted are valuable even with this in mind.

[154] Archer E Schook et al., "45-Year Trends in Women's Use of Time and Household Management Energy Expenditure," *PLoS One* 8(2), 2013.

To the virtuous woman desiring marriage to a good, godly, and successful man, know this: Whatever you do for your husband to free his time, to release him to accomplish, to send him into the world hungry to succeed, ready to sacrifice to provide for his family, you will receive rewards in return. The man leading a loving, calm, and organized home can accomplish much. All men will fritter away some time, some men will waste much time, but the worthy man, the one you're looking to marry, will generally put it to good use, redounding to the benefit of you and yours for a lifetime and beyond.

To the good man, without setting aside God's mandate to love her well, understand that you will never be the perfect husband, and it's not within your control (nor is it even your place) to meet all of her needs, as unmet needs keep us, both men and women, dependent upon our good God. *A person absent of need wouldn't be following or seeking God.*

Summary for a happy marriage: Become a good and capable man, and marry a virtuous woman who is happy being a woman.

RAISING YOUR DAUGHTERS

For you know that we dealt with each of you as a father deals with his own children, encouraging, comforting, and urging you to live lives worthy of God, who calls you into this kingdom and glory.[155]
— The Apostle Paul

A young, attractive woman should eschew the attentions of the hoards, for their motives are generally bad and their actions tend to inflate the woman's ego sufficiently that she often overlooks, or even rejects, indications of commitment from a moral man, thinking, "It will wait." Not so. For a woman, time is the enemy. Instead of basking in shallow male attention, she should earnestly seek the life-long love of one good man, for his love will enhance her life forever, while those who chase the wind inherit the wind.

Though this book has focused on helping men navigate the tricky waters of the LSR culture, it should be apparent that the same lessons apply equally well to young women. Many of the women

---

[155] 1 Thessalonians 2:11

who fall into the LSR trap have "daddy issues," not enjoying a good relationship with their fathers. Be a quality role model for her, helping her form a healthy model of the marital relationship by observing a father who loves his wife and children well and leads intentionally. Such models are best built over time, starting from childhood, and are best inculcated when observed in daily life. A woman blessed with an authentically Christian father will be prepared to easily discern the counterfeit man from the genuine article. Love her, hug her, play with her hair, tease her, touch her face, talk with her, read to her. You are her God-given protector, teacher, and guide.[156] If you build a proper relationship with your daughter, you'll also become a model of what she'll be seeking in a husband. As you examine your life from this perspective, the love you have for your daughter will naturally motivate you to become a better man.

> *Many women have waited for five or more years for commitment that was never to be given but, mark this, almost always having provided sexual access during those waiting years.*

This is important because your daughter needs your guidance and counsel even more than your sons. She will reach her peak sexual market value at a younger age and will maintain it for a shorter period of time. She must use those few years of peak SMV

---

[156] In like manner, men, engage in regular physical contact with your sons. They need to feel your strength and need to have physical contact just as much as your daughters and, outside of athletic pursuits, moral touch is often hard to come by for teenaged boys. Hug him firmly, bump chests, wrestle with him, and by all means rub his head. No one but a dad gets away with rubbing a teenaged son's head.

well, working to attract quality men, rapidly ascertaining their willingness to commit, and moving on if timely commitment is not forthcoming. Many women have waited for five or more years for commitment that was never to be given but, mark this, *almost always having provided sexual access during those waiting years.* Those making decisions while panicked tend to make poor decisions, so though her time frame is compressed relative to men, you should encourage her to move purposefully while seeking to live with the joy and peace that only comes by trusting God.

Teach her to guard her sexual access gate carefully to both attract a good man and to encourage him to open his gate of commitment and invite her in. In referring back to that ever helpful law of supply and demand, the lower the supply of a good in relation to the demand for it, the higher the price that must be paid. Just as the rare flawless diamond stands in stark relief from its much more numerous flawed counterparts, the rarity of chastity preserved in an LSR culture is *extremely* attractive to a wise and moral man. True chastity isn't merely stopping short of full intercourse, but is also a state of mind, a woman intentionally reserving her body and her affections for her future husband: "So they are no longer two, but one."[157] Though it should go without stating, a Christian woman should never consider marrying a man who's not a Christian: "Do not be yoked together with unbelievers."[158] The Apostle Paul provided direct advice to young widows - advice that is applicable to any single woman - when he wrote: "But if her husband dies, she is free to marry anyone she wishes, but *he must belong to the Lord.*"[159] No Christian should even entertain the thought of marrying outside of the faith. It's a well-trod path, one full of anguish, a veritable river of tears. The marriage bed is not the place to schedule an evangelical crusade. At the same time, many a man genuinely lives

---

[157] Mark 10:8
[158] 2 Corinthians 6:14
[159] 1 Corinthians 7:39

for his God without wearing a WWJD bracelet. You must observe and act with discernment.

I cultivated and continue to enjoy a wonderful relationship with my oldest daughter, Jacy. During her teen years we spent many hours together discussing what was before her – the opportunities, the temptations - and what she might do to successfully navigate those tricky waters. During those years I wrote her numerous letters, notes, and cards. With her permission I am sharing a few of those letters throughout the rest of this chapter. If you are like most, upon reading this chapter and the letters, you'll find my tactics well out of the mainstream for today's world. Over the years I have received some complaint and criticism for my methods but the best part of being a man of conviction, I simply do not care what others think or do. I simply did what I believed was right and Jacy eventually embraced her daddy's protection wholeheartedly, basking in it, for she absolutely knew that I loved her and was seeking the best for her. It wasn't about me. My other two daughters will benefit from Jacy's experience as we learned what worked and what didn't. May your daughters benefit too.

The Christian man is called to do his best to raise his daughters well, *in spite* of the LSR culture in which we reside. Though it will be challenging, do not stand aside, dad, while your daughter is tempted, pushed, and prodded into immoral sexual activity. America has gone full LSR, the low sexual restraint culture now waxing from sea to shining sea as it feeds upon our sinful nature, already at its apex in our inner cities, with the rest of America following the plume.

Historically this is nothing new. Ours is far from the first nation to succumb to the LSR culture and, barring our Savior's return, it won't be the last. It's just that cultures don't long survive on an LSR binge. Sodom may have been the pinnacle LSR culture in all of ancient history, but she and her sister city were only small outposts compared to America. Yet how many virtuous women lived there?[160] Probably none! Sodom's fathers were too busy satisfying their animal lusts to even care about their daughters. Today's inner cities are little different, imprisoned or otherwise absent fathers leaving daughters without dads and teenaged boys running rampant absent a father's strong but loving hand for guidance and restraint.

While she was in college, my daughter Jacy served as a volunteer counselor at a crisis pregnancy center. One young inner city mother, age fourteen, was literally startled when Jacy advised her that it would be in her best interests to avoid further sexual activity until she was married, that, in the meantime, she should just say no. This fatherless young child responded, "I didn't know I could say no." This young girl is living in a culture no different than that of Sodom. May God and His followers help her and her myriad sisters of all creeds and colors. Most receive no guidance or protection from their fathers; don't unwittingly let your own daughters join them.

> *...the Enemy knows that virginity given in marriage strengthens the marital bonds and wishes to destroy that bulwark thoroughly before her marriage is consummated.*

As your daughter is maturing she will hear many voices that stand in stark contrast to yours, for the Enemy knows that virginity given in marriage strengthens the marital bonds and wishes to destroy that bulwark thoroughly before her marriage is consummated. You must equip yourself to guide her with authority

---

[160] Genesis 18:20

and a father's love, to hold sway. Our culture is awash in sexual stimulation, the goal to trigger and hold people in a constant state of sexual arousal. In an informative and oddly applicable study by Charmaine Borg at the University of Groningen, it was found that women who were sexually aroused were more willing to perform tasks that might be deemed disgusting.[161] Sex is no doubt messy and weird, initially disgusting for most when its secrets are first revealed. This disgust factor may well have helped women protect their chastity in other times, but in a sex-obsessed culture intentionally creating constant sexual arousal in both men and women, those protective disgust responses fall by the wayside, many times at a very young age. You will do well by her to limit her exposure to such stimuli.

Protect your daughter always. Do not stand aside and allow the wolves to encircle her. (And you know they are wolves!) As I have previously shown, when faced with a desire-reason dilemma, a woman relies on her emotions much more heavily than a man. The wolf will take full advantage: "Come on baby. Everybody's doing it and I have to. We need to. I love you. I'm going to die. Don't deny me your love. Don't deny me your love!" [her sexually aroused emotions override her reason] "Yeah baby, that's it! Oh baby, you feel so good. Wow! Oh baby, baby, baby!" He takes her virginity, step one to wrecking her future marriage to another man. She probably cries from the pain before the act is even over, but the Enemy celebrates, and the wolf is satisfied if only for the moment. She regrets but will return again, to him and likely others, and pregnancy is only a matter of time. Most women who find themselves in this pressure cooker will succumb, so keep her far from it.

---

[161] Eddie Wrenn, "So that's how they put up with men! Study finds sexually aroused women are less easily disgusted," *Mail Online*, September 13, 2012.

Once you identify a potential wolf, outthink him. Any social pecking order is only valid in its particular context, so the alpha male role is always situational. For example, only about five percent of the over one million high school football players ever play in college, and the pros draft only a miniscule two hundred and fifty-five players a year. That high school star chasing around your daughter with his alpha cred in tow probably won't ever play a single down in college. He's not Joe Flacco, so give your daughter a proper perspective. Belittle him a bit. I'm not suggesting you harm the potential predator, just keep him well-heeled, for a woman will not willingly have sex with someone she doesn't respect.

When Jacy was in her first year of high school I was walking through her school gym in suit and tie and saw just such an opportunity. I seized it. The sophomore boys were performing two-armed free weight curls using absolutely horrible technique. I stopped at their group and explained the proper technique, instructing them that, in order to extract the full benefit from the curl exercise, they needed to raise and lower the bar slowly, thereby strengthening their arms through the full range of motion, not cheating by using the momentum of the bar to make it easier to start the lift. One of them tried the exercise with proper technique but had too much weight on the bar to do it right; without the bar's momentum he could barely even get started and then failed utterly. Being the good man that I am, I stepped in to demonstrate, grabbing the bar and showing them all the proper technique, intentionally performing the exercise with just one arm as opposed to their two, raising it very slowly while using my other arm to point and instruct them during the entire demonstration, thereby providing irrefutable proof of my vastly superior strength. I put the bar down and instructed them they'd be better off reducing the weight until they'd built their strength a bit and then walked away, every single one of them knowing beyond a shadow of any doubt that I was fully capable of crushing them like bugs should the need ever arise.

(Warning: When you initiate such a lesson, make 100% sure that you can pull it off or it will have the precise opposite effect. By all means, work to build and maintain your strength; however, if you weren't endowed with a strong physical body, creatively apply your particular gifts and abilities to the same effect.)

You can bet that I found a low-key way to make certain Jacy found out what had taken place, making sure that she knew her most likely potential ~~boyfriends~~ wolves were mere little playful puppies. That's how you do it, men: Actively cultivate your daughter's respect for you, and annihilate any respect she might have for a potential wolf. Will the wolves hate you? Not if done well and with a smile, but do you really care what they think when you thwart their designs on your daughter? The sex act is the ultimate submission for a woman. If she doesn't respect a man, she will not voluntarily have sex with him, ever. Note that once a good and godly man appears on the scene, you'll need to reverse course and begin slowly and carefully building her respect for him as his commitment level increases.

> *The sex act is the ultimate submission for a woman. If she doesn't respect a man, she will not voluntarily have sex with him, ever.*

Early on Jacy and I established that anyone who wanted to take her on a date had to come to my office and visit with me first. I was as friendly as a dad can be in these visits but they were full of straight talk, right down to demonstrating the parts of my daughter they could touch (a very short list) and the parts that were forbidden. At the end of each visit I handed them the following letter:

May 29, 2003

Dear Wolf Puppy (just kidding),

I wanted to write you this note so that we could develop an understanding of the responsibilities you accept when interacting with my daughter. This will help make sure there is no confusion about my expectations. First, know that Jacy is a much-loved, delightful young lady. At some point, she will make some lucky man a wonderful wife and companion.

Until that time my God-given responsibility is to protect and nurture Jacy, a responsibility that I take very seriously. One of my goals (and Jacy's) is to have Jacy enter her marriage with no regrets or apologies. God's plan for marriage is "one man and one woman" and we must seek to honor that during our premarital days. Today, God's way and our culture's way are in direct conflict. I challenge you to seek and follow God's path in your relationships. Our popular culture says sex (any kind of sex) is great. God says that sex outside of marriage is wrong and has many negative consequences. He created sex for His good purposes but warned us to enjoy it only within the bounds of marriage.

From all accounts, you seem to be a solid young man, blessed with many talents and abilities. As you no doubt know, Jacy enjoys your company very much. Because of this, you are in a position to bring her joy but you also present her with danger - spiritually, emotionally, and physically. To that end, as you and Jacy spend time together, I request that you keep the following points in mind:

1. *While you are with her, her safety is your responsibility.*
2. *Seek to keep yourselves accountable and <u>around other people</u> at all times.*
3. *Always, always be a perfect gentleman. (I'll be asking her if you have been.)*
4. *Time apart is very healthy for both of you.*

5. Seek to honor God in all aspects of your relationship.

Remember, by faithfully following these guidelines, you not only honor God today, but show proper respect for your future wife and Jacy's future husband, whoever they might be.

Please feel free to talk to me at any time - day or night - if you have any questions about what we've discussed today.

Sincerely,

In addition to protecting your daughter from potential ~~boyfriends~~ wolves, it's extremely important to cultivate and enable her friendship with other girls committed to living a biblical lifestyle. When a young woman (or man, for that matter) is standing in opposition to an entire culture, even a single friend standing alongside can add incredible reserves of resolve. "Two are better than one, because they have a good return for their work: If one falls down, his friend can help him up. But pity the man who falls and has no one to help him up!"[162]

Spend time, effort, and energy teaching your daughters what to look for in a man. *They know nothing of men.* Help them. Make sure that in choosing marriage, she's selecting a husband for life. It's easy to follow a good man, torture to follow a fool. This is no inconsequential choice.

You also must be honest with her that men are initially attracted to physical feminine beauty above all. Some women are naturally more attractive than others. Help her do an honest assessment regarding her looks and encourage her to look her very best. There are good men at every level of physical attractiveness, and women

---

[162] Ecclesiastes 4:9

are no different. If a girl is born homely, there is no need for shame, just as there is no reason for conceit in the attractive girl, since none of us had any role in our basic looks. However, I've seen numerous girls who weren't presenting themselves at anywhere near their potential. If your daughter is overweight, encourage her to slim down. In today's overweight world, a young woman of proper proportion stands out from the crowd. If she doesn't understand the relationship between nutrition, diet, exercise and weight, by all means help her. Encourage her to wear her hair long. This is not complicated from a physical perspective: God wired men to be extremely attracted to long locks, feminine faces and curves, then made women curvy from every possible angle of observation. A slender woman has no straight lines! Think about that for a moment: feminine faces curve, buttocks curve, legs curve, breasts curve, the sides of her torso curve, her hair often curls, even her neck often curves, plus, as an added bonus, she's soft to the touch. A shapely woman simply radiates in a man's eyes, drawing his attention. Do you think it an accident that sports cars are designed with curves, that men enjoy driving fast on curvy roads, and that even female cartoon characters are drawn with exaggerated curves? It is how men are wired. Ladies, let me give you straight talk too: Excess weight greatly reduces your attractiveness. So do eating disorders that make women too thin, so don't go overboard; however, as in most things, a balance must be struck, but most women today need to lose weight.

    The virtuous woman should never make the mistake of flaunting her curves. She doesn't need to! It's quite possible to radiate beauty while also being modest, as immodesty sends all the wrong signals: "Like a gold ring in a pig's snout is a beautiful woman who shows no discretion."[163] You should seek to strike the balance of being attractive without instigating sexual arousal in a man. In today's

---

[163] Proverb 11:22

world, men already have enough sexual temptation to navigate without you adding to their burden.

As a corollary lesson for the young men: You will occasionally run across a woman who's naturally attractive but not disposed to makeup and some of the finer points that most women use to stand out. I went to high school with just such a woman: Smart, sweet, pretty, a lovely figure, and a cheerleader. But for some reason all the boys of the high school saw her as their sister, not as girlfriend material, so she did not date anyone to my knowledge and was notably absent at the various dances. I lost track of her shortly after graduation and next saw her at my ten year reunion. She was simply lovely, appeared to have had married extremely well, and was living a very high profile life. How could all the young men have missed her potential? I do not know, but I make this observation: Should you encounter such a woman, she will more likely be a virgin and will genuinely appreciate the attentions of a good man. I am sure my former classmate is a superb wife and mother.

To help Jacy choose wisely, I wrote her what turned out to be a very long letter, considering each and every word, and presented it to her just past her 19th birthday. We studied it together. I give full permission for you to use this letter, in whole or in part, with your daughter. May your daughters enter their marriage pure of mind, heart, and body. May they each love well, marry well, and bless you with many grandchildren.

July 8, 2005

Dearest Jacy,

Outside of your decision to follow Jesus, making a good decision about whom you marry will mean more to your life and your children's lives than any other decision you will ever make. As your father, I have been put here to help you make a good decision.

God created women and understands your need for romance, love, leadership, and protection. Pray to Him that He will provide you a God-fearing man to fulfill your needs. At the same time bear in mind that <u>no man can satisfy all of your wants.</u> Much as too much money or comfort drowns out God's voice, so too would the perfect husband. God declared it so; otherwise, we might forget about our dependence upon Him. Still, God holds marriage up as the model for the relationship He desires with His church, as He outlines in Ephesians, Chapter 5, and that is a good and healthy model, one worth emulating.

Marriage can be a source of great joy but never think for a moment that marriage is a perfect fairy tale. God stated in Proverbs 27:17, "As iron sharpens iron, so one man sharpens another." Marriage and children are perhaps the ultimate sharpening tools in God's hand, helping us to become more like Jesus; however, sharpening and honing requires friction and is not always, or even usually, a pleasant process. Deep and restful sleep is but a dream for a new mother!

<u>Your first and foremost task in marrying a good man is becoming and remaining a woman worth marrying:</u> following Jesus with all your heart, remaining pure, and keeping yourself naturally attractive. One of my goals was to get you through the teen years without a list of regrets a mile long. That doesn't mean that you can't or haven't made decisions that you'd like to change; no one but Jesus himself could make that claim. But, rather, I've hoped and prayed that you would traverse that potentially tumultuous period without harming your ability to live the balance of your life as God would have you to live it. In that regard, I commend you. God has blessed you for your faithfulness and will continue to do so. In fact,

your very actions and decisions have surely encouraged His blessings.

How do you best live in a state of singleness? You should seek to live a joy-filled single life each and every day, casting aside your anxiety by handing it to the Lord. As your friends marry you may begin to sense that you're somehow falling behind, missing out. This simply isn't so; though there is little reason to wait once you've found the right man there should be no race to marry. In fact, some He has called to a life of singleness, either for a time or for a lifetime, a state where your life can be completely dedicated to His purposes and His preparation. Whether or not singleness is God's long-term plan for you, it's imperative that you seek to remain joyful in your singleness, remembering that God is the ultimate husband. A desperate woman (or man) makes poor marital decisions and then lives a life of misery, filled with regret. At the same time, keep in mind that many a woman has passed up a very good man in wait for the perfect only to find herself never married though it was her complete desire. Do your best to maintain continual faith in Him regardless of your current circumstances.

Now let's unpack this and get very practical. To be wed to a virtuous man, you must first meet him so use your creativity. Work to be slim and attractive while remaining modest, for God wired men to be very attuned to feminine beauty. Good men want to marry a virtuous woman.

Pray for your future husband every day of your life; you might consider the following:

1) *You don't know the identity of your future husband but I believe God does. Pray that he will honor God in his singleness; pray that he'll be protected from pornography; pray that God will prepare his heart and mind for you and*

your children; pray that God will instill in him a love for God and God's people. Pray that God will reveal a life-long, clear-cut purpose in life for your husband, for purposeless men are easy targets for Satan.

2) *Pray that God will bring you together and, if it's the Lord's will, give him, you, and both families conviction that marriage is a good and proper course. Pray for help in establishing a firm foundation in His will and for His blessing on your future union.*

3) *Should you encounter a possible husband, pray for clear and honest eyes. During your courtship, pray that God will protect you both from intimacy before marriage. I can provide you all manner of studies and statistics if you desire, but trust it's God's plan and know that it's critically important to establishing a marriage on a firm foundation. It takes a firm decision and unwavering commitment to enter a marriage chaste, but the life-long rewards of doing so are worth all of the effort and all of the sacrifice. <u>Trust is always strongest when it's never been broken</u>. Know that the whirlwind of passion impairs one's good judgment, so be ever diligent.*

Now to analyze the man: God always provides tools to discern, two of the most important being His Word and direction from the Holy Spirit. When examining a man as a potential husband, I think Paul's requirements for a church leader are a most excellent place to start, for the following passage describes a man whom God would entrust with His church, His flock. A man worthy of such great trust would certainly be a man eligible for marriage. In 1 Timothy, Chapter 3, Paul states the following:

"Here is a trustworthy saying: If anyone sets his heart on being an overseer, he desires a noble task. Now the overseer must be above reproach, the husband of but one wife, temperate, self-controlled, respectable, hospitable, able to teach, not given to drunkenness, not violent but gentle, not quarrelsome, not a lover of money. He must manage his own family well and see that his children obey him with proper respect."

Let's explore these characteristics:

1) *Above reproach - Reproach means to bring into discredit. A man who is above reproach cannot be discredited. He is what he is and he is authentic, the same at home, at work, or on a Friday night away from home. He has nothing to hide, even under close scrutiny. In short, he is full of character. This phrase is all-encompassing; a man possessing all of the other characteristics mentioned in this passage will, by definition, be above reproach. To be "above reproach" allows one to live without fear of anything or anyone and is engendered by a healthy fear and awe of God. This is the only passage in the entire Bible that uses this phrase.*

2) *Husband of but one wife - I believe this means more than the obvious. In my mind I see this as a man dedicated to his wife beyond his own personal wants and desires, even his own life. He will treasure his wife as a gift from God. Such a man is kind and courteous to all but will never allow courtesy to be misinterpreted for more. If another woman shows an interest in him, he will either leave or will respond by talking about the love and devotion he has for his wife. He will never denigrate his wife. If you find such a man, cherish him and take care that you don't unintentionally take advantage of his love and devotion.*

3) *Temperate - God is balanced; He has things under control. Likewise a temperate man is of an even keel, not given to excesses. He is steady, not erratic. He is the anchor in the midst of the tempest.*

4) *Self-controlled - He is slow to anger and doesn't lose his self-control even when angry. When others are losing their head, he is still thinking rationally.*

5) *Respectable - Such a man does what is good in God's eyes and is worthy of respect. A respectable man sets a good example and is worthy of emulation. This should be given its due because the wife is commanded to respect her husband. Know that it is all but effortless to respect a good husband and beyond impossible to respect the unrespectable.*

6) *Hospitable - A hospitable man makes others feel comfortable, welcome, and valuable. He attends to other's needs before his own. He sees people through God's eyes and welcomes them without regard for their station in life, for a waitress is just as valuable in God's eyes as a president or a king.*

7) *Able to teach - Being able to teach has two requirements: First, he must have something worth teaching; he must possess knowledge and wisdom. Second, he must be able to relate his wisdom in ways that others can understand and adopt. This doesn't mean he has to be a dynamic public speaker or a fabulous communicator, though it's fine and perhaps best if he is. Rather, it means that he is capable of transferring his knowledge and wisdom to others, whether they're little children, his wife, a colleague, or a total stranger. He well remembers that he is to bring up his children in the fear and admonition of the Lord. And a good*

teacher is always curious, a good listener and an ardent learner.

8) *Not given to drunkenness* - This doesn't mean that he doesn't drink wine (though many Christians do abstain), but it does mean that he never drinks to excess lest he forfeit his self-control.

9) *Not violent but gentle* - You may have seen men spoiling for a fight. Many times they are drunk with alcohol. A worthy man will never look to violence for fun or entertainment. In fact, he will use all prudent means to avoid violence; however, left without option, he will defend his family with all effort and without regard to his own safety. Still, as long as it's possible, he will remain a gentle man in every respect, a gentleman. I like Papa's simple statement of this philosphy, "I treat them as well as they'll let me."

10) *Not quarrelsome* - A virtuous man is a peaceful man. He gives no reason for argument. You'd have to be looking for an argument to find one and, even then, he would use his wisdom to defuse the tension and restore peace.

11) *Not a lover of money* - Money is simply a marker for earthly resources. If I have a hundred dollar bill, that gives me the right to deploy a hundred dollars' worth of resources in any manner I see fit. Controlling significant resources gives one the ability to help build God's Kingdom; however, if one lacks wisdom money can become the worst of traps. Proverbs states that, "The blessing of the LORD brings wealth and he adds no trouble to it." P.T. Barnum has an interesting take, "Money is in some respects life's fire: It is a very excellent servant, but a terrible master." Possessing resources can be a blessing, but we can never let resources

replace our dependence upon God Almighty. The way a man spends his resources (his time and money) reveals much about the man. You should look for a man who is prudent yet generous with his resources.

Looking beyond this great passage, it's an observable fact that women prefer strong men and, were I a woman, I would happily pray for a strong, determined husband with good leadership skills, a man who leads men. What sane woman would desire to marry a weak man, though I suppose the weak need wives as well. But I must hasten to add this caution: Women are so naturally drawn to strength that it often clouds their judgment as to character. You, being a woman, are naturally so disposed; therefore, in this matter, in addition to praying for eyes to see, it's imperative that you also seek counsel of learned and trusted men who know your prospective husband. Though both are good, <u>strength without character makes a horrible husband.</u>

> **Women are so naturally drawn to strength that it often clouds their judgment as to character.**

No man is perfect but, much as a fine wine improves with time in proper storage, so a good man improves himself with age and experience; therefore, provide your future husband the great courtesy of taking into account his youth and inexperience. Even a young man of utmost character still has much to learn and many mistakes to make before he's honed into God's final form.

I hope this helps Jacy. You are a wonderful daughter and bless me greatly. I am very proud to be your father. I encourage you to stay close to God and be worthy of the man God described through Paul. When God brings him to you, you will be greatly blessed, as will he, as will your children and your descendants for generations, should the Lord tarry. And God will be most pleased and will bless your union. Still, it is my hope that it'll be years before this man enters your life, but prepare now. May God bless you and keep you my beloved daughter.

Love,

Daddy

Here it's appropriate to pause for a paragraph and speak specifically to the single Christian woman who is past her peak SMV, desires to be married with her whole heart, but it just hasn't happened, thousands of *seemingly* unanswered prayers eroding her faith. Though there are other categories, I am speaking specifically to the woman who's lived a virtuous life but Mr. Good Enough has never arrived or has never been willing to commit. Or maybe you set aside Mr. Good Enough in order to seek Mr. Better, but he never came. It matters not. My dear lady, continue living a joy-filled single life. God truly uses those refined by suffering, and living life with unfulfilled dreams is a form of genuine suffering. At the same time, there are many good men who have found themselves thrown into the divorce court's maw, men whose dream of having a faithful wife was destroyed by the woman herself. Some will be damaged goods but many will recover and be capable of being a fine husband. But know this: He will likely be loaded with external baggage and court orders that will divert significant resources to his deserter, especially those men with young children. This baggage cannot be overemphasized and will cause you pain and at least some discord. Even knowing this, I would prayerfully consider such a man if it's in your heart. Both he and his children would benefit greatly from having a good and godly woman in their lives. Your sister's silly and short-sighted hypergamy may ultimately redound to your great benefit. A used car can still be an excellent car.

As your daughter approaches marriage you will do her and her future husband a great favor by continuing to invest in both of them, reminding them of their biblical roles and responsibilities in their future union. However, once she's married, you must purposefully restrict yourself from active intervention. *Do nothing to undermine the respect your daughter has for her husband.* If she has questions or concerns, answer them and encourage her without demeaning her husband. If her husband asks for advice, by all means, dispense it gracefully and with all tact. Otherwise, just bite your tongue until it bleeds. Seriously. All marriages have issues to work through. If she chose well, they'll work through them just fine. Though she'll always be your daughter, in marriage you have given her to another man. He must increase and you must decrease.[164]

I wrote the following letter to encourage Jacy as a young mother because being a young wife and mother is one of the hardest roles to fulfill well on the face of this earth. The grind of caring for a helpless baby builds character possessed in no other way. In mothering well, she must literally surrender herself daily to God. Paul states it well, "But women will be saved through childbearing – if they continue in faith, love and holiness with propriety."[165] When the rest of the culture undermines motherhood, find ways to remind her of its eternal importance. Remind her of God's command to Noah and his sons, freshly off the ark: "Be fruitful and increase in number and fill the earth."[166] Mothering well is worth doing and will earn many heavenly crowns. In fact, I believe it possible that good and godly mothers will merit among the greatest heavenly rewards.

---

[164] John 3:30 (NASB)
[165] 1 Timothy 2:15
[166] Genesis 9:1

Dearest Jacy,

In the post-modern world that we live in people are looking for their validation in all the wrong places. As Christians we should look for our value and validation in His Word. The Word is the Truth.

Here are some points for you to consider. First, both men and women have been assigned responsibilities in this life and the wife is to submit to her husband. Looking at more of the relevant Scripture gives us a fuller picture.

The husband is called to the following:

1) Love his wife: Ephesians 5:25, Colossians 3:18
2) Be not harsh: Colossians 3:18
3) Be considerate to his wife: 1 Peter 3:7
4) Respect his wife as the weaker partner: 1 Peter 3:7

Conversely, the wife is called to respect and submit to her husband. This does not make the wife into a slave, certainly not for any woman who marries well. I believe we've discussed this before, but it can perhaps be best understood with an illustration from Star Trek. Captain Kirk is the captain and Spock is the First Officer. The FO has the right (nay, the duty) to weigh in if he believes the captain to be incorrect or ill-informed. A good captain will seek out the advice of his trusted FO. The FO has full authority to direct anyone on the ship but the captain unless it violates a direct order from the captain. If there is a decision to be made upon which the captain and the FO cannot agree, then it's the duty of the captain to make the decision and the duty of the FO to follow the captain. This arrangement preserves order and fosters agreement. Two captains under the same circumstance would eventually destroy the ship, fighting each other and not the Enemy! Additionally (and importantly) under those hopefully rare circumstances of disagreement, it's the captain that holds the full responsibility for his decision, good or bad. Spock is valued; his contributions are significant; the ship needs him; the captain needs him; the crew depends on him; he is important![167]

Do not forget that these roles are purposeful earthly roles Jacy, not eternal. No one is married in heaven. In fact, the Apostle Paul wrote, "You are all sons of God through faith in Christ Jesus, for all of you who were baptized into Christ have clothed yourselves with Christ. There is neither Jew nor Greek, slave nor free, male nor female, for you are all one in Christ Jesus. If you belong to Christ, then you are Abraham's seed, and heirs according to the promise."[168]

Understand this well: You are directly a daughter of the Father through Christ. This position does not depend upon your husband but, rather, upon Jesus drawing you to him and you accepting his offer of eternal life with him. That relationship was in place before you were married!

Still, God is a God of order, not disorder.[169] *To minimize discord and promote unity, God has given us these rules while here on earth, along with numerous other guidelines. This is not the order in heaven for there is not marriage in heaven*[170] *and no slavery, certainly not to a human master. We all have rewards and important roles to play both here and in heaven; Scripture tells us*

---

[167] Credit to blogger and author Athol Kay for the Star Trek analogy upon which I built, more widely recognizable and more easily understood than the obscure historical example I'd used previously. As an atheist with a good sense of humor, I'm sure he'd be amused that I adapted it to illustrate Christian principles in my letter.
[168] Galations 3:26
[169] 1 Corinthians 14:33
[170] Matthew 22:30

we will judge the angels.[171] Jesus told us that the "last will be first."[172] I don't know precisely what that looks like, but I know it'll be glorious and joyful since "God will wipe away every tear from [our] eyes."[173] In the meantime, we're called to hold and strengthen the fort (the Church) and our families. God has made you perfectly for your role in His Kingdom, both now and on the other side.

Remember that God's rules aren't to tear you down but are for the well-being of his people. Without good families and mothers, civilization dies a horrible death. God wants us to multiply!

The lies of the "isms" are from the Enemy. We must seek the Truth. And from your comments, I know that you are. And yes, you are quite smart and funny and fun to be around and loving and wise and lovely and sweet and considerate and a whole bunch of other good and delightful things. I am blessed to have such a daughter; your husband is blessed to have such a wife; and your children are blessed to have such a mother.

Love,

Your Proud Daddy

Raise her well, dad! Eternity depends upon it.

---

[171] 1 Corinthians 6:3
[172] Matthew 19:30
[173] Revelation 7:17

TRIAGE

1730: A vision without a task is but a dream. A task without a vision is but a drudgery. A vision and a task are the hope of the world.
— Inscribed upon the wall of a church in Sussex, England

Don't be discouraged. We're in the people business and the people business is a messy business.
— Pastor Joel Atwell, as spoken to the author

Over the past twenty years I've had the opportunity to teach and counsel with a significant number of men in various states of marriage or career difficulty, or those just wanting to mature in their faith. It's been one of the blessings of my life to witness prayerful and careful counsel improving lives and marriages. There is a deep satisfaction in witnessing a man breaking free from his chains, stepping up to life's plate with grit, determination, and resolve, and his wife happily responding to his leadership. An oversexed man is a happy man.

Conversely, it's utterly heart-wrenching to witness the pain inflicted by divorce. Divorce goes against God's creation, being an inherently brutal and destructive act. It's not surprising that God hates it. The open and public and complete rejection by your spouse inflicts grievous wounds, often throwing both sides of the former whole into poverty, while simultaneously requiring emotional support to children and others who are impacted, drawing on non-existent reserves. It is extremely trying, even for the initiator. Yet even in such dire circumstances, God will minister: "He heals the brokenhearted and binds up their wounds."[174]

With but a few exceptions, the men with whom I've counseled married women with known risk factors that, taken collectively, should have dissuaded the informed man from making the marriage commitment in the first place. Very few men have been taught those risk factors, maleducation and misinformation being the norm. With the combination of ignorance and the pursuit of sexual gratification driving them, men often make poor marital decisions. This book seeks to banish such ignorance and shine the light of truth on the matter, for an informed man makes better decisions, at least has the ability to make better decisions.

There are always signs and cues that a woman is considering divorce, some subtle and some shouting from the mountain tops: open and constant discord, increased attention to appearance, expressed approval of friends divorcing, decreased sexual response, open disrespect towards her husband, a surprise decision to return to school to fulfill goals never before expressed, and so forth. A sign of particular note is if she becomes suspicious or, particularly, if she openly accuses you of misdeeds of which you're completely innocent. It's not unusual for a woman illicitly involved to become suspicious of her husband: After all, if she's not trustworthy, how

---

[174] Psalm 147:3

could her husband be trustworthy? Sin clouds one's judgment. The psychologists call this projection.

If you sense your marriage is troubled, by all means seek to save and improve it. Even if you chose poorly in marriage, you made a lifetime vow before God. Oftentimes the best means to foster improvement in your marriage is to improve yourself, concentrating on what's fully within your control, the "plank in your own eye,"[175] and striving to become a godly man, a strong man, a man's man, the best man you're capable of becoming:

1. Follow and obey your God. *Know His Word.* Seriously men, how Christian men so routinely ignore their God and His Word boggles my mind. We're not 15th century peasants purposefully kept ignorant by the church priests and with no recourse. Today, we have resources available at our fingertips of which our forebears could only dream, making biblical ignorance completely voluntary. Knowing His Word is important because a man genuinely walking with his God will become more like Him over time: strong when necessary, gentle when possible, wise and discerning always. Follow Him; seek His will: "Always be prepared to give an answer to everyone who asks you to give the reason for the hope that you have."[176] I understand that some men find it all but impossible to wade through Scripture and, indeed, the Bible can be confusing, especially until you become familiar with biblical history; however, any man can get direction from God by reading and studying the wisdom literature: Psalms, Proverbs, and Ecclesiastes; and every man will benefit from studying Jesus' own words in the four gospels: Matthew, Mark, Luke, and John.

---

[175] Matthew 7:4
[176] 1 Peter 3:15

2. Spend time thinking about what you must accomplish in this life. Prayerfully construct a mission plan to meet those objectives and then doggedly pursue it with all meekness, meaning strength under control.

3. Spend time with other authentically Christian men. This can be a Bible study, pickup basketball, shooting sports, rehabbing a needy family's home, camping in the mountains, riding a mountain river, golfing, anything that puts you shoulder-to-shoulder with other Christian men. Spending time with good men will sharpen you, refresh you, encourage you, and improve your marriage.

4. When facing challenge of any sort, endeavor to step into the challenge, meeting it head-on. Do not be too proud to seek godly counsel when you need it.

5. Become a student of the godly, successful leaders in your midst. Study them and learn, even to how such a man stands, his bearing, how he carries his hands, how he interacts with others, how he acknowledges another in passing, how he interacts with women. For example, a leader's hands seem perfectly content to dangle on the ends of his arms without need to find a home until they're needed. Examine, adopt what you can, and make it your own. Over time you can become comfortable with such changes. Another example of some interest: When two men are passing, they often nod at one another in acknowledgment, just a friendly gesture. A follower tends to nod his head down while a leader tips his head back. Which do you do? Practice the latter. But don't let your analysis stop at the mere physical markers; seek to understand the substance of the man. If there is a man whom you particularly respect, ask for his counsel. By limiting your request to a defined period you will significantly

increase the chance of his accepting. Buy his morning coffee twice a month for six months and learn. He may decline; if he does, ask another. But you may find yourself pleasantly surprised. I currently lead a mixed Bible study on Monday evenings, read the Bible with another man on Tuesday evenings, participate in a men's Bible study on Wednesday mornings, and meet individually with a younger man very early on Thursday mornings. Oftentimes the most effective ministry happens one-on-one or in small groups. His investment in you will bring him eternal rewards. Be courageous. Ask.

You'll need time to make these changes and you likely have it available. According to Nielson, the average American watches over thirty-four hours of television per week.[177] If you're the average man, turning off the television in your home will free up enough time to make major changes in your life and in your family. I possess almost no knowledge of any television series produced in the last twenty years, actively choosing ignorance in television entertainment, as I put those hours towards other purposes, trying to spend sufficient time performing what Stephen Covey characterized as Quadrant II activities, important but not urgent.[178] I used to greatly enjoy playing and watching God's own game of football and still watch an occasional game, but now that it's a penalty merely to make a good hit - even when wearing the obligatory pink shoes - I'm losing interest there too and gave up my season tickets for the local team several years ago. Time is very limited and the wise man will carefully prioritize his time in accordance with his mission and his responsibilities.

---

[177] "State of the Media: Trends of TV Viewing – 2011 TV Upfronts," The Nielson Company, 2011, 11/3079, (www.nielson.com).
[178] Stephen R. Covey, *The 7 Habits of Highly Effective People* (New York: Simon & Shuster, 1989), page 151.

Most troubled marriages are sexless, sometimes for years on end. If you find yourself in a sexless marriage, you are far from alone. Life happens, but such situations don't often manifest themselves overnight, instead developing one step, one decision at a time. Do not let this pattern develop in your marriage as it's the beginning of the end. As you've read earlier in this work, the sex act is one of the most submissive acts a woman performs, allowing a man access to her inmost parts. If your wife doesn't respect you, a regular sex life is but a dream. As this chapter's opening quote suggests, let's assign some tasks to help the sexless man transform his dream into hope. First, recall once again that Christian marriage is a lifetime commitment. Do not follow the world's way and throw your marriage away when things get tough. The couple who sticks together through tough times tends to become happier over time. In fact, one study found that, "*Two out of three* unhappily married adults who avoided divorce or separation ended up happily married five years later. Just one out of five of unhappy spouses who divorced or separated had happily remarried in the same time period."[179] Stick with it; analyze what's transpired. She responded to you at one time so, unless it was a sham marriage, she found you attractive in the past. What happened? While thinking this through, remember what women find attractive in men. Have you let your SMV slide beyond the natural aging process? If so, that's the first place to start.[180] This will take time, energy, and money. Do it. And I must hasten to add, though it's not any big secret, there is absolutely no need to inform your wife what changes you're *going* to make. Changes are much more effective if she notices the results

---

[179] Linda J. Waite et al., *Does Divorce Make People Happy?* (New York: Institute for American Values, 2002), page 5.

[180] I highly recommend Athol Kay's book, *The Married Man Sex Life Primer*. Though Athol does not approach this subject from a Christian perspective, I trust that a mature man can separate the wheat from the chaff in what is, on balance, a very helpful book on raising one's SMV.

of her own accord. Actions do indeed speak louder than mere words. As you increase your SMV your marriage will likely improve.

If you're in a sexual drought, here are a couple of ideas that you might find helpful to reestablish the sexual relationship: Strength is attractive, and you are both stronger and faster than your wife, likely well beyond her belief. Being physically weak, she simply has no idea the strength you possess, and it's hard to demonstrate this differential from the recliner. I remember Jacy asking to arm-wrestle me one day. She tried one arm: fail. Her two arms against my one: fail. She finally wrestled my arm with her leg and, if I recall correctly, both legs: fail. Your wife has no idea of your relative strength, and this is knowledge you wish her to possess, so look for a natural way to demonstrate. Look for an appropriate moment, simply lift her off the ground and kiss her. Hold her there and look into her eyes. Make it look effortless. If you are incapable of doing this, start working out, or get her on a diet, or both.

> *What woman can resist a man throwing lead, smelling of gunpowder, fully capable of protecting her in a dangerous world?*

Strength commands respect; respect encourages submission; sex is submissive for her. Let's connect the dots, men. Along the same vein, if you are a competent shooter, teaching your wife how to properly handle a firearm will both increase her ability to protect herself and will establish a teacher-student relationship, naturally increasing her respect for you. Guns being dangerous, a man handling them well must be a little dangerous too. See how this works? What woman can resist a man throwing lead, smelling of gunpowder, fully capable of protecting her in a dangerous world? The more dangerous her present circumstances, the more attractive such a man becomes. Creating a written self-defense plan (or a storm plan or fire plan) for your household and practicing it will also reinforce your leadership and build respect. It's also a smart thing to do for your family. This same advice works well for the single man: A shooting instructor (or dance instructor, exercise coach, and so forth) meets some pretty ladies. I'm just saying.

Marriage counseling is a good idea for the troubled marriage, so long as you're seeing a biblically-based counselor. If you're a Christian, there is absolutely no reason to seek counsel from an equalitarian feminist of either gender. A churchian equalitarian feminist might even be worse since you'll get the same bad counsel but with an air of biblical authority. There are many churchian counselors who counsel based upon their university indoctrination while their Bible gathers dust on their desk. No counsel is preferable to bad counsel.

If you've begun meeting with that strong, godly mentor I suggested above, there is some likelihood that his wife could counsel yours: "Likewise, teach the older women to be reverent in the way they live, not to be slanderers or addicted to much wine, but to teach what is good. Then they can train the younger women to love their husbands and children, to be self-controlled and pure, to be busy at home, to be kind, and to be subject to their husbands, so that no one will malign the word of God."[181] If you need help, ask for it. But always step into your problems, facing them like a man.

If your wife files for divorce, immediately seek godly counsel. If it's possible to save your marriage, by all means, save it. If she refuses, realize that she has just declared war on you and will be

---

[181] Titus 2:3

employing the courts to control you, remove your kids, and put you in divorce slavery. Find and engage the best legal counsel available and use every means to preserve your financial assets and secure custody of your children. To ensure clarity, I shall state what should be obvious: *Once she steps out from under your umbrella of protection, she is no longer under it.* Do not become complicit in her sin. Do not help her! Her car have a flat? Too damn bad. Let her figure it out. If she's in an unsafe predicament with the kids, go pick up the kids, but you no longer have *any* obligation to protect her from herself or anything else. When you solve the wayward wife's problems, you're further enabling her to destroy, not only your marriage, but your children. Albeit a slim chance at that juncture, letting her immediately experience in full what life is like without a protector is probably your last chance to save your marriage. Let your pastor know what's going on. If a well-intentioned churchian helps her, let him know that he's enabling the destruction of your marriage. There are times when it's quite biblical to withhold assistance. It's called tough love.

> ***Once she steps out from under your umbrella of protection, she is no longer under it.***

Realize that your former lover is now your biggest enemy, her future lovers the most likely people in the world to sexually abuse your daughters. Most states have sex offender registries; you should check out any man your wife is involved with against these registries. Private investigators can provide you a criminal background check for a reasonable fee. Your children are innocent and deserve your protection and precedence in all your decisions. Concentrate on your children as they'll need your guidance more than ever. Many kids will feel guilty, thinking their parent's divorce was their fault. Make certain to actively banish such thoughts from their minds.

If you find yourself in divorce slavery, pray that God will help you live a joyful single life. If you believe it within your right to remarry, do not seek to interact romantically until you're in a place where you can be content to live as a single man, *at least a year* after the divorce is final. You are wounded; you are likely broken. Seek healing. In the meantime, improve yourself.

It is great irony when a woman's hypergamy drives her to divorce a good man, as she most often ends up with a lesser man, usually a string of increasingly lesser men, while her former husband recovers and, if he remarries, usually marries better in every respect. Female divorce hypergamy is a logical failure of immense proportion, her completely uncoupling natural consequences from the decisions that brought them to be.

Above all, if you find yourself navigating these tricky waters, remember your children. God help us. Remember your children. Always remember your children. They are deeply wounded. Be their rock in the tempest. And point them towards your Rock.

CONCLUSION

When the foundations are being destroyed, what can the righteous do?[182]
— King David

When plunder becomes a way of life for a group of men living together in society, they create for themselves, in the course of time, a legal system that authorizes it and a moral code that glorifies it.[183]
— Frédéric Bastiat

Great nations rise and fall. The people go from bondage to spiritual truth, to great courage, from courage to liberty, from liberty to abundance, from abundance to selfishness, from selfishness to complacency, from complacency to apathy, from apathy to dependence, from dependence back again to bondage.
— Alexis de Tocqueville (Credit disputed)

---

[182] Psalm 11:3

[183] Frédéric Bastiat, *Economic Sophisms* (New York: Foundation for Economic Education, 2002), originally written in 1848, Second Series, chapter 1, page 130.

Conclusion

I hope reading these chapters has refined your worldview, increasing its accuracy. A man living in obedience and genuinely seeking truth pleases God: "But seek first his kingdom and his righteousness, and all these things will be given to you as well. Therefore do not worry about tomorrow, for tomorrow will worry about itself. Each day has enough trouble of its own."[184]

In Samuel Adams' speech before the formal signing of the Declaration of Independence, he stated, "If ye love wealth better than liberty, the tranquility of servitude than the animating contest of freedom, go from us in peace. We ask not your counsels or arms. Crouch down, and lick the hands which feed you. May your chains set light upon you, and may posterity forget that ye were our countrymen." What a man. Regrettably, America's former liberty, for which so many paid so dearly, has been squandered and we now live in a culture spiraling down by almost any measure. Most pertinently for the subject of this book, we're inarguably living in a full-blown LSR culture, a significant predictive marker of a culture's doom in and of itself. On de Tocqueville's scale, as a society we are clearly moving from apathy to dependence and major segments of America are fully prepared to accept bondage, so long as it's a comfortable bondage (always promised but never fulfilled.) Any society that sets aside its God in pursuit of man-made idols and their attendant worldly pleasures either repents or is destroyed.

The widely held moral fiber present during America's founding has long since vanished from ubiquity, now residing in but a remnant. America's future is not bright, her decline evident in myriad ways: Her moral decay, the rot of her cities, the loss of her manufacturing industries, her families failing, her unsustainable debt load a veritable Sword of Damocles, her bankers counterfeiting her

---

[184] Matthew 6:33

currency, her future commitments to her citizens impossible to keep, the growing dependency of her populace, the corruption of her leaders, the undefended invasion of her borders, her love of liberty extinguished along with Lady Liberty's torch. Yes, it is sad, even tragic, particularly given the heights she had attained, likely the greatest social experiment in all history. People lived well and attained much. The Founders (sans but a few) must be honored and history informed. Almost to a man, they sacrificed for posterity, many while serving their God. Hopefully the next generation seeking spiritual truth will learn from America's failures and liberty will prevail once again if our Lord tarries. Never forget Jesus' promise that he will build his church and "the gates of hell shall not prevail against it."[185] Gates are defensive in nature, meaning that God's Kingdom (that includes us) must be on the offensive, attacking the Enemy's fortifications.

> *If God has blessed you with exceptional abilities, don't rest easy in them. Put them to work, blazing a path for others, giving them their "chests," planting seeds of liberty in a remnant that may someday rise again.*

But what are we, as individual men, to do in such times? All is not lost even when living in a declining culture. Dominant nations rarely die overnight, and America won't either, for even an unopposed invasion takes time. Use this time to prepare and teach, for it's always possible for the wise and considered man to live a more worthy and impactful life than would that same man had he been content to live in ignorance and haste. Become the wisest, most knowledgeable man you can become. If God has blessed you with exceptional abilities, don't rest

---

[185] Matthew 16:18 (KJV)

easy in them. Put them to work, blazing a path for others, giving them their "chests," planting seeds of liberty in a remnant that may someday rise again.

Invite the Potter to form your clay, even with a *heavy hand,* for God often trains his warriors in the wilderness. Follow Him. Seek eternal perspective. Live on a mission. Continually thank Him for your many blessings. Learn. Love. Marry well. Suffer well. Pray often. Laugh even in misery. Observe. Think for yourself. Enjoy. Fail. Succeed. Seek wisdom. Live free. Teach your children well. Look forward to hearing those proverbial words which every Christian should strive to hear, "Well done, good and faithful servant! You have been faithful with a few things; I will put you in charge of many things. Come and share your master's happiness!"[186]

If I speak in the tongues of men and of angels, but have not love, I am only a resounding gong or a clanging cymbal. If I have the gift of prophecy and can fathom all mysteries and all knowledge, and if I have a faith that can move mountains, but have not love, I am nothing. If I give all I possess to the poor and surrender my body to the flames, but have not love, I gain nothing.

Love is patient, love is kind. It does not envy, it does not boast, it is not proud. It is not rude, it is not self-seeking, it is not easily angered, it keeps no record of wrongs. Love does not delight in evil but rejoices with the truth. It always protects, always trusts, always hopes, always perseveres.

Love never fails. But where there are prophecies, they will cease; where there are tongues, they will be stilled; where there is knowledge, it will pass away. For we know in part and we prophesy in part, but when perfection comes, the imperfect disappears. When I

---

[186] Matthew 25:21

was a child, I talked like a child, I thought like a child, I reasoned like a child. When I became a man, I put childish ways behind me. Now we see but a poor reflection as in a mirror; then we shall see face to face. Now I know in part; then I shall know fully, even as I am fully known.

And now these three remain: faith, hope and love. But the greatest of these is love.[187]

In this passage, it's easy to focus on what's obviously important: faith, hope, and love; however, there is more, much more. Thinking people oftentimes ponder about how things really are, but we are informed that even Paul knew only "in part," yet someday we shall know fully. Rest easy knowing that, in God's good time, the Christian man will know fully!

And now I leave you with my personal mission, one which I keep in the forefront of my mind by reading it nearly every single day:

1. To love and serve my God with all my heart, mind, and spirit.
2. To love, cherish, teach, care for, and provide for my wife and my children.
3. To serve my fellow man with my time, talents, and treasure.

This book exists because of my mission, my God not letting me rest easy until these words were written. May He use them.

If you don't have that invaluable wise father or grandfather, let me close by standing in but for a moment, to pronounce a blessing upon you:

---

[187] 1 Corinthians 13:1

Conclusion

"Be strong and courageous…Be strong and very courageous."[188] *May you find and live for your mission. May you love well. May you change eternity for the better. May you put yourself in Bondage to God's will and nothing else, so that you may live free. Live free, my brother. Godspeed.*

"By their fruits ye shall know them."[189] Choose the Red Pill. Always choose the Red Pill. By all means, always seek the Truth!

---

[188] Joshua 1:7
[189] Matthew 7:16 (ASV)

www.ingramcontent.com/pod-product-compliance
Lightning Source LLC
Chambersburg PA
CBHW031356040426
42444CB00005B/314